BEYOND THE LIMITED AWARENESS OF YOUR EGO
YOU ARE BEAUTIFUL, YOU ARE VALUED, YOU ARE
ENOUGH AND YOU ARE LOVED UNCONDITIONALLY

Dancing
with the Ego

BERNICE M. WINTER

BALBOA.
PRESS
A DIVISION OF HAY HOUSE

Balboa Press books may be ordered through booksellers or by contacting:

Balboa Press
A Division of Hay House
1663 Liberty Drive
Bloomington, IN 47403
www.balboapress.com
1-(877) 407-4847

Because of the dynamic nature of the Internet, any web addresses or links contained in
this book may have changed since publication and may no longer be valid. The views
expressed in this work are solely those of the author and do not necessarily reflect the
views of the publisher, and the publisher hereby disclaims any responsibility for them.

The author of this book does not dispense medical advice or prescribe the use
of any technique as a form of treatment for physical, emotional, or medical
problems without the advice of a physician, either directly or indirectly. The
intent of the author is only to offer information of a general nature to help you
in your quest for emotional and spiritual well-being. In the event you use any
of the information in this book for yourself, which is your constitutional right,
the author and the publisher assume no responsibility for your actions.

Any people depicted in stock imagery provided by Thinkstock are models,
and such images are being used for illustrative purposes only.
Certain stock imagery © Thinkstock.

Printed in the United States of America

ISBN: 978-1-4525-7052-5 (sc)
ISBN: 978-1-4525-7054-9 (hc)
ISBN: 978-1-4525-7053-2 (e)

Library of Congress Control Number: 2013904471

Balboa Press rev. date: 12/31/2013

The stories in this book are true. This book was inspired by the author's life and is a response to many requests for a written work after she shared excerpts of her life in conversation or in seminars.

This book contains opinions, conclusions, and theories that have worked for the author but have not been tested on other people. The author does not represent herself as an expert on any topic other than being who she is. The suggestions and exercises in this book are based on her experiences, which she shares for readers to use at their own discretion. She encourages readers to seek professional support if they so desire, since each individual has unique needs and a singular journey. The author, the editors, and the publisher of this book take no responsibility for any impact or outcome that may result from the contents.

I dedicate this book to my mother with appreciation, recognizing the pain and anguish I caused in banishing her from my life during the years that I blamed her for my problems, when in truth the pivotal choices that impacted my life were actually mine. I understand that she did the best she could with what she knew, as did I. I now know better, so I am able to do better. I love her dearly and am grateful for having her in my life, since it was because of her that I discovered who I am.

Table of Contents

Foreword

～～～～

Life comes with its challenges and getting beyond them can seem insurmountable sometimes. We often look to our past and decide how to create our future from that perspective. We may look to the future with great apprehension as we try to figure out how to live life differently—how to create the life we have been dreaming about—but fear seems to hold us in place. The greatest challenge most of us face is to be present with what is and to leave the past in the past. What we must understand is we are not the people we were last week and we are not the people we were last year. Because of the experiences we have had, our perspective on life has changed; therefore, we are different. Living in the past with our new perspective doesn't work. It doesn't appear to be moving us in the direction we have been seeking, and yet many of us continue to live in this fashion. More important, our past wasn't all that good in the first place, so why would we choose to repeat it? Seems silly, doesn't it? The truth is we are creatures of habit, and learning something new can seem to be a daunting task. Fortunately, you are in the right place and reading the right book.

Bernice M. Winter has shared her journey with you in the hopes that your life may be easier. Bernice experienced an extremely difficult childhood, and her adult life reflected all that she had learned. Needless to say, it was a mess. Having struggled financially, experiencing failing health and relationships that were, well, destructive and abusive, Bernice has moved past all of this and created a successful and fulfilling life for herself. The journey she took was arduous, yet she gained powerful insights that brought profound and lasting change in every area of her life. She has created success for herself, and in this book she shares with you insights she learned along the way.

I have known Bernice through her healing journey, and I can assure you this book is a clear and concise account of that journey. As her friend, I found it difficult to watch the struggles she was experiencing, but more importantly I must say that the sadness I felt for her quickly changed to awe as I watched her overcome all of these difficulties and create magic in her life and in the world. You have made a wise decision to read this book. Step it up a notch and do the exercises she suggests. Knowledge without action is really nothing at all. Use this book as a guide to your dream life. And please remember that you are fully capable of living your dreams not someday but now.

In Joy,
Barbara Schreiner-Trudel,
Author of *30 Days to Joy*
www.joyhereandnow.com

Bernie- Dancing With the Ego

Imagine yourself standing perfectly still. Suddenly, without any provocation your inner ego steps out and takes on a life of its own. It tells you to ignore the dance, to not laugh, to disregard the direction your heart leans toward. You are compelled to stay only in the past. You are told, "do not discover the newness that seeks to discover you."

Dancing With the Ego sets the stage to recognize two parts that make up your present. You and your ego stand face to face. Your ego stands as a calculating search engine for the data of life experiences you have compiled over years. Your ego is there to remind you of the years of life experiences. The ego will inform you of your capabilities and your inabilities.

You are standing side by side with your ego. Do you choose to dance, or will you choose to sit this one out?

When dancing you will need to determine who this partner is. You will sift through the words, feelings, and thoughts that jump out at you. You will be challenged to accept who your ego has become. You will be challenged to begin a series of new steps reprogramming your past. You will be challenged to displace the past with a present that informs a new direction.

As you dance you will stumble, you will step forward. You will change positions. You will give direction. You will lead or you will be lead. Your ego will dance with you, against you, along side of you, away from you. At all times being unseparated from you.

A dance style will emerge, a new confidence will hold you tightly understanding a new opportunity is emerging. You will be invited to the next dance fully knowing this is just the beginning of more to come.

While reading Dancing With the Ego, you are being invited to look at yourself, imagine your ego as your dance partner. You are asked to recognize the many facets of a dance knowing that it is the dance of life that emerges. Who you are, who you become, how you present yourself, how you choose not to present yourself will all affect this dance.

So turn on the music. Dance till your heart can be joyful. Dance till the new becomes newer. Build on what has been learned from the past. Do not ignore your ego, just do not let it lead.

If one follows the metaphor, many good things can be learned. At the same time the metaphor is not meant to be the template for life. Just like life, the well laid plans of life break apart.

Important questions arise from the similarities and the differences of the metaphor. The invitation does not stop with the dance. The dance encourages each of us to discover ourselves in an environment that nurtures and builds us along the way.

I have known the author for many years. Her heart genuinely invites you to dance with her. She invites you to dialogue with your ego. She invites you to moments of self discovery. She invites you to moments of renewed enthusiasm. She invites you to discover the joys of the past, the hurts of the past, the strengths and weakness that will allow to peek into a future that could be yours.

Carl Deline

Acknowledgements

~~~~~~~~~

It is not easy to find words to express appreciation for everyone who helped bring this book to life. It is the result of support from a team of amazing people. Without their aid and feedback, *Dancing with the Ego* may not have become a reality.

I would like to acknowledge and thank the people who contributed their unique talents to ensure this project came to be.

I am eternally grateful to Barbara Schreiner-Trudel for encouraging me to write this book. For better than fifteen years, she persisted in asking me when I would do it. Without her friendship, support, and consistent belief in me, I may not have stepped out of my comfort zone and put my thoughts on paper. I also thank her for writing such a heartfelt foreword.

Many thanks to Barbara, Lorraine Williamson, and Crystal Fawkes for the many hours they spent editing every word of every chapter.

Heartfelt thanks to Barbara, Lorraine, Jasi Aujla, Tim Cyr, and Gerald Gjerde for reading this manuscript in its early stages and encouraging me to publish these words. Their comments touched my heart ...

"I was honored to be asked to be one of the proofreaders on this book. What I didn't expect was that it would profoundly affect my view of myself and how I see the world."

—Lorraine Williamson

"Bernice M. Winter shares an intimate, and a very heartfelt, recounting of the many lives she has lived in the journey of her lifetime. The interweaving of fairy tales is beautifully done to draw connections that spark new awakenings of awareness for each of our own life journeys."

—Tim Cyr

"This is one of the most powerful, self-awaking, thought-provoking, and self-healing reads. A real soul-wrenching, self-help, raw, powerful guide. A journey awakening your inner spirit to find pure love, peace, and happiness in your life."

—Jasi Aujla

Chapter 1

THE EGO IS WHO YOU THINK YOU ARE

*Be careful how you are talking to
yourself because you are listening*

—Lisa M. Hayes

This quote by Lisa Hayes reminds us that we are listening to our self-talk. We develop opinions about who we are as we collect data during our everyday experiences. We listen at many levels and absorb data from many sources, around the clock. Although we are not aware that we are listening, we are taking in information at an astounding speed. We are often not consciously aware of the information we are absorbing, yet that information is what our ego identity draws on, as we live each day.

I would like to demonstrate this by sharing the story of a little girl who was sent to live with her aunt and uncle for the first few years of her life.

Then when she was roughly three years old and her father had been released from jail, she returned to live with her parents. Her father was an alcoholic and a heroin user. Her mother was overwhelmed by life and angry much of the time.

Her father took this little girl to the bars with him and prostituted her, starting when she was three and continuing until she was a young teen. Her mother constantly called her a tramp, told her she was ugly and useless, and said she had better pray that some man would want her when she grew up.

The girl loved to spend time with her dad and played guitar with him. Her dad liked to laugh and sing and was not angry and mean like her mother.

Her mother scolded her for being a daddy's girl and made her serve the men booze and clean up after the wild parties. When the girl complained, her mother would often put her in a closet or a dirt cellar, telling her she needed to think about her disobedience and bad behavior and be grateful that she had a home. The family moved from one abandoned building to another. This meant changing schools every few months.

The mother sent the girl to work cleaning houses on weekends when she was eight. When the girl no longer wanted to knock on doors and clean houses, her mother made her live on the streets, telling her to learn to appreciate the good home she had.

At fourteen, the girl got a job and helped her family pay the bills. As the eldest of five, she continued to care for and support her siblings while living on the streets. She felt there was less violence there than in her home.

She was told that she was not smart enough, that there was not enough money for her to continue her education, and that school was a waste anyway, since girls just got married. She was reminded daily that her biggest problem was that she was a dreamer and that expecting she could achieve an education fed the side of her that would not accept reality.

At twenty-one, this young woman was sharing her days with bitter, frustrated people who expected to be shortchanged by life.

Would you agree that this was not an ideal childhood? Do you think that this girl was disadvantaged and that she would likely be limited in life? Do you think she had a strong sense of self-worth? Would you expect her to be confident or to need guidance? Do you think it highly unlikely that this girl could grow up to be a healthy, confident, and contributing adult without a lot of therapy?

I can assure you that this girl did not surrender to the limitations set by her parents and her childhood experiences. In fact, this child is now a confident and respected woman whom people admire and trust. I can assure you of this because this is my story, or at least a snippet of it.

If you are saying "wow" or feeling a sense of awe, then I would like to introduce you to your authentic self. It is your genuine self that felt awe and joy that this child did not fall into the cracks of society or become an abuser or a drug addict. It is your ego that is surprised, shocked, and doubtful that this is true. Your ego may be suggesting that there must be a catch, something that is not being said or perhaps being exaggerated.

Our ego tells us that surviving such a devastating childhood is highly improbable and quite rare—especially without therapy, counseling, or rescue. When your ego tells you it is not that simple and you agree, you do not put a lot of faith in your ability to change or make much effort to do so. If you want to change your life but agree with the limited awareness of your ego, you can be sabotaged, confused, challenged, and insecure. You may feel that you cannot trust your own thoughts.

I have repeatedly experienced this obstacle. It took me many years to understand that the reason I felt stuck, stupid, and hopeless was not because my mother told me these things as a child, but because, forty years later, my ego was still reminding me of these words. For years, I questioned how I could be affected for a lifetime by the words and experiences of my early years when I had no choice but to be where I was. I walked away from that environment forever at twenty-one.

From where I sit today, at fifty-eight, my first twenty-one years were a mere blip in my life. My intellect told me it made no sense that these years should have a grip on me, yet my life's experiences were textbook for someone with my background: betrayal after betrayal, disappointment, heartbreak, loss, bankruptcy, divorce, sabotage, homelessness at forty, cancer, allergies, poor decisions, repeated cycles, and many, many tears. With thousands of volumes of information to consume, I was relentless, intent on figuring out how something that happened to me so many years ago, something out of my control, could have such a hold over me for a lifetime. I read, listened to speakers, attended seminars, studied, did all the homework, and followed the suggestions. I even broke a one-inch-thick piece of wood with my bare hand during a seminar on developing self-confidence and breaking barriers. I did it without hurting myself or drawing one drop of blood! Each time my hopes were dashed. As I faced bad news or another disappointment, I would curl up and cry. In my darkest despair, I felt useless and unwanted, unloved, and frustrated.

Still, I could not accept that I deserved a life sentence of loneliness, despair, and worthlessness. I could not imagine that any child could be born with such a black cloud hanging over her. I clung to the belief that like all people, I was born lovable, valuable, and beautiful. I was convinced that we all have the right to be loved, cared for, and respected, to be happy even if our family members are not happy. I also understood that with free will we all have the right to make choices, and I believed, as I endured my childhood, that when I turned fourteen I would be old enough to make those choices and no longer be restricted by the anger and neglect that ruled my home. I knew as a child that if I stayed alive, kept my wits about me, and remained clean (no sex, drugs, or alcohol) I could one day be a businesswoman with an education and a happy family.

That dream is what kept me going as I maneuvered past the obstacles blocking my road. I had never thought that it would take this long or be such an interesting journey. At fourteen, my view of what I needed to succeed was simplistic. Despite the many challenges, I blossomed into the woman I am proud to be today. To achieve this, I had to face many things about myself and who I thought I was, including the limitations imposed by my ego. The final step that brought me to the place where I now live as my authentic self, as the person I knew existed when I was a child, was learning to dance with my ego. I hope you will embark on this journey with me and learn to dance with your ego. I hope that in sharing what I discovered along my path, I can help you create shortcuts on yours. My greatest desire is for you to feel free to live as your genuine self—to live as who you were born to be before the world interfered with the perfect you.

Post these words where you can see them every day: Beyond the limited awareness of my ego, I am beautiful, I am valued, I am enough, and I am loved unconditionally.

Chapter 2

DANCE PARTNERS FOR LIFE

*God wisely designed the human body
so that we can neither pat our own
backs nor kick ourselves too easily.*

—Author Unknown

Thousands of books are available to help us make choices as we maneuver through life. We must live by many expectations and rules if we want to be viewed as successful, spiritual, balanced, healthy, wholesome, and beautiful. We devour tips on how to make career and fashion choices, on what foods are healthy, on how to make friends, how to choose hobbies, and how to be interesting. We can't overlook pointers on how to remain youthful and, most important, on how to attract a soul mate. There are volumes on selecting among candidates for life partner. Add to this the hundreds of books on what to do when we change our mind (or heart) after concluding we have chosen the wrong partner.

Support is available for those who feel they were shortchanged because of family members or career choices and believe their opportunities are limited. There are tips on how to make it through these minefields and overcome life's many challenges. Close, loving, storybook families are the envy of those who feel disconnected from their relatives, so people with family envy issues need pointers as well. There are also thousands of books on business and wealth. Get rich now, but if you don't, there are support groups. Name the cause, and someone has developed a program, written a book, or set up a foundation to deal with it. Once a problem is labeled and categorized, someone will create a support group. With all of the blogs, e-newsletters, e-libraries, and online coaching available, we should have no problems or worries. We can find the evidence to show that we are not to blame for our challenges, losses, disappointments, or confusion. With all this awareness, information, and support, why is it that people of all ages continue to ask, "Who am I? and "Am I happy?" People spend hours of time and billions of dollars searching for their purpose on earth and billions more trying to improve or fix who they are.

Why are we not happy and feeling fulfilled, secure, and loved? We have followed the rules and have all the toys and trappings that prove we are successful, so why are we not elated? Is it possible that our authentic, original self is lost beneath a mountain of information too overwhelming to sift through? Is it possible that when we say we are lost or feeling out of sorts our genuine self is pleading to be heard?

We select our partners by dating and spending time getting to know them before making a commitment to be with them, whether for a second date or for a lifetime. Why do we take so much time exploring a potential mate, yet spend no time getting to know who we are? Knowing who you are is the foundation for success in life. When the cabin pressure on an airplane changes, you are told to don your own oxygen mask before putting on your child's. Your genuine self needs to be nourished, protected, and heard. Give your inner self oxygen first, and then find out who you are. Getting to know who you are is critical to a life of success, freedom, joy, and peace. Most of us go from one experience to the next, never stopping to ask if we like who we are or if we even know what we do or do not like. Do we know what makes us feel good, secure, valued, and loved? Do we know what will make us sad, insecure, or lonely? I have learned that it is just as important to know ourselves and to choose the attributes we desire in ourselves as it is to evaluate prospective partners and friends. When we learn how to know and honor our genuine selves, we can stop searching for answers and live in the moment, experiencing life to its fullest in whatever way brings us meaning.

When we mindlessly go from day to day, experience to experience, without considering how our genuine self feels about things, we allow our ego to lead us in whatever direction it desires at the moment, without thought or question. Our ego keeps the facts about who we are present in our awareness. These facts are based on what we learn as we go through life. If we were told when we were six years old that we couldn't do something, our ego will hold that idea forever, or until we give the ego new information. Our ego is essentially our pilot through life, our source for self-reference. Our ego stores and accesses our failures, mistakes, hurts, fears, doubts, anxieties, and all those things we felt from childhood until today. Our ego also stores our successes and any new information that we accept as true for ourselves.

It is immaterial to the ego that it doesn't know how to manage the many thoughts and emotions accumulated over a lifetime. The ego does not rationalize or think; it simply stores data. As we grow older, our ego does not clean out the files it keeps; it changes the information only when we give it new data. From birth to adulthood, we spend most of our time collecting data on what hurts us, what scares us, what makes us laugh, what tastes good, and what makes others happy, angry, or sad. All this is collected and stored in our ego. When we react to an experience, the response comes from our ego. We all have an ego. We can't live without one. Egos are as individual and varied as people are. We say that some people have big egos; we think of them as being "full of themselves." We see others as having small egos and admire their humility. This tells me that egos are not cast in stone. The ego is adaptable and will change when the information it is given is updated. With this in mind, we should carefully select the information that we want our ego to store. Because the ego is our awareness of who we are, if we want to experience peace, love and happiness, the information our ego holds must accurately represent who we are. If the awareness of who we are is held by our ego, should we not agree with who and what our ego holds us to be?

To get a better understanding of why the ego self can be so different from the authentic self, I looked up the definitions for *authentic, living, self, ego,* and *genuine* in the Webster's and Oxford dictionaries.

Webster's Dictionary:
• Authentic: adjective—to be "genuine"
    • Living: adjective—having life; pertaining to existence; the condition of being alive; the means to support life
    • Self: noun—the distinct identity and individuality of a person
    • Ego: noun—the conscious self
    • Genuine: adjective—authentic: sincere and honest

Oxford English Dictionary:

- Authentic: adjective—of undisputed origin; genuine

  - Living: adverb—at the time of something's occurrence

  - Self: noun—a person's essential being that distinguishes them from other people; a person's particular nature or personality

  - Ego: noun—1) a person's sense of worth and importance; 2) the part of the mind that is responsible for the interpretation of reality and a sense of personal identity

  - Genuine: adjective—authentic; able to be trusted

Put together:

  - Ego: a person's conscious awareness of worth and importance

  - Authentic self: genuine; the distinct identity and individuality of a person; a person's essential being that distinguishes him from other people; a person's particular nature or personality

  - Authentic living: genuine; having life; pertaining to existence; the condition of being alive; the means to support life; at the time of something's occurrence
    Authentic self: the distinct identity of the individual person
    Authentic living: the condition of being alive, with the means to support one's individual life

Based on these definitions, it stands to reason that the conscious awareness of a person's self-worth, the data stored in the ego mind, is not authentic in and of itself. It is the genuine self that can be relied upon to hold the truth about a person's distinct and individual identity.

With so many definitions of the ego, including "Edge God Out" or "the part that makes us human," I wanted to be sure of my theory about the relationship between our ego and our authentic self. These definitions support the idea that everyone has an ego and that the ego holds our definition (awareness) of our perceived self-worth. Our ego makes us human; it is where the facts supporting our personality, presence, and identity are stored. So, if we need an ego to have an identity, why is there such a disconnect between who we genuinely are and who our ego perceives us to be? The answer is key to resolving the question "Who am I?"

We all know that our spiritual self is beautiful and complete, the way God made us, and that it is politically correct to say, "I am beautiful," "I am wealthy," or "I am creative." We have learned the value of repeating these statements as affirmations and mantras, yet the core self often resists believing these ideas. Our ego challenges these affirmations with every thought. Drowning out the voice of the ego with chanting and affirmations may work for some, but not for all. You must be determined to find the method of reprogramming your ego that works for you, and when you find it, you must embrace it, be grateful, and use it!

When you add the law of attraction to the awareness that you feel challenged in some way, you will invite events that confirm the ego's awareness, reinforcing the challenge in this area. This will always appear to be true for you in that circumstance until the ego has new information to draw on. Several different approaches may be required to replace the information held by your ego. The key is to know that the information stored is not cast in stone and can be changed. Your job is to find the program to rewrite the data in your file.

For the many years that I felt unwanted and worthless, I attracted people who betrayed me. I trusted one longtime friend completely and believed her when she said she wanted to take charge of her life. She was sixty-one and financially dependent on her ex and her children. I offered her a position in my company, paid her while she was being trained (which I did not typically do), and after fourteen months she quit, blamed me for her challenges, reported me to the labor bureau, and hired a lawyer to sue me. She then got a job in the same industry, thanks to the free training, and never spoke to me again.

On another occasion, I took a chance and hired a gal who had been fired from her last position. After several years of working for me, she sought to open her own company, providing the same service. Over a one-year period, she transferred my databases and templates to her home computer. She commingled the accounting between my two companies, and I was fined $14,000 by the government. She spread rumors, saying that I was dying of cancer, that I had sold the company, and that I had moved out of the city. When I discovered this, terminated her with cause, and refused to make her last salary payment, she challenged me with the labor agency. The police would not file charges against her, since all the data was transferred electronically. Our company lawyer said the woman would have to be put on notice that if she used the templates or contacted the clients in my database, she would be charged. Within twenty-four hours of my terminating her, she had sent announcements to my clients and had her company registered. My lawyer said she had paid for legal advice on how to do this and stay under the radar. I lost $80,000 in revenue due to her sabotage. My company didn't fully recover until 2007. The rumors are still popping up on the Web, and years later I run into people who are surprised that I am the owner of my company.

Since that time, there have been three other occasions when I made special allowances for people and they betrayed me and used me. My low self-esteem was the catalyst for these experiences. When I realized I was attracting these people because of my core beliefs about myself, I changed the way I did business and lived my life. I was amazed at how quickly things turned around once I had this clarity. I became aware that it was my ego that felt I was unwanted and that each time I made a decision I instantly began preparing for the worst. Recognizing the law of attraction at play, I saw how I sabotaged myself in relationship after relationship with my focus on the negative. People didn't stand a chance with my determination to find the worst in them!

With a new awareness, it becomes critical to the goal of living authentically that you pay attention to what the ego holds and filter out what is not true for you, leaving the genuine self as the ego's awareness of who you are. When this is achieved, you will automatically live the authentic life you seek, filled with peace of mind and happiness.

To take the lead as you dance with the ego, it is imperative that you sift through the mountain of information that the ego holds in your conscious and unconscious personal awareness. You must decide how to live your life and choose what is stored in the ego's data banks. You can become aware of the things that support who you genuinely are, or you can allow yourself to be led by the expectations of your ego. If you have thoughts of should and should not, maybe and can't, then this list of your favorite excuses is readily available in the awareness that your ego holds for you. If this is the case, relax, because knowing this about your ego is the first step toward releasing the genuine you. The ego is not in charge. You are—if you're willing to take charge.

My hope is that you are reading this book because you want to live each day authentically.

The goal is to be in a respectful partnership with your ego, not to tame it, dismiss it, love it, or ignore it. Knowing who you genuinely are allows your ego to hold the facts that you choose to have filed there. These updated facts will be available to you in your ego data bank as you experience each day, resulting in harmony with yourself and helping you to live fully as you were born to do.

There is only one you and only one dance for you and your ego. You cannot be separated from your ego, and your ego cannot be ignored. It does not negotiate or think. Your ego is simply a storage cabinet where you have been keeping your valuables since you were born. Think of it as a computer or an iPad. You have folders in directories that contain a vast amount of data obtained from many sources. When you want to access a file, you simply go to the directory, open the file, and retrieve the information. The computer doesn't tell you what to do with the information. It takes instructions from you. It may prompt you to correct spelling or tell you that a file is not available at the moment, but it does your bidding. When you delete a file, it is because the file no longer has value. When you create a file, the new information is now readily available just as the information stored for ages was. The computer doesn't care if the file is new or old. It simply retrieves the information you request. This is comparable to the role of your ego: it holds the data you have collected about who you are and makes the information available whenever you seek it.

This dance can be a slow dance, an awkward dance, a two-step, or a fast-swinging polka. Your genuine self and your ego must work in unison to find the rhythm that flows uniquely for you. It is your dance, not mine, not your parents', not your boss's, or your partner's. It's yours and yours alone. You choose the music, the tempo, and the vocals. The music is in you, activated by your energy, thoughts, beliefs, and actions.

The goal is to allow your genuine self to take the lead. To do this, you must become mindful of who you are, what you like and do not like, what makes you smile, what brings you tears. All facets of you are included. You may get stepped on or lose your balance for moments, days, or more. That is okay. This is only a dance, one experience followed by another, and when it flows it is wonderful. Dancing through uncomfortable and awkward moments will give you insight, and these moments of feeling out of balance often open the path to the next step. You must allow the dance to flow at a pace that works for you, since this is all about doing what honors the authentic you, now ready to become visible.

Chapter 3

Be Aware of the Land Mines

It's not who you are that holds you back;
it's who you think you're not.

—Attributed to Hanoch McCarty

Be aware and sensitive to the signs that you are repeating patterns, reliving old experiences, feeling stuck or stale, doubting yourself, feeling out of sorts or blue. If you feel you are in a rut and going nowhere, take note that this is a conversation you are having within yourself. These are the perceptions your ego has filed on your behalf. This is the data that you are using to validate your decisions and actions. These land mines set off reactions and perpetuate the cycles that keep us feeling stuck and out of control.

I took several steps to defuse my land mines and take back control of my life, allowing me to lead the way, even when a twist or turn appears. Make this the day you decide to reprogram your ego, take charge of yourself, and claim the leading position in your life.

Although updating the files held by your ego is similar to deleting or overwriting a file in your computer, the operator, namely you, may not have the skills or knowledge to complete this task. The good news is that, as with all things in life, what we don't know we can learn and develop with the proper tools and support. The ego is not the enemy, nor is it easily willing to swap old information for new. There is a bit more to it than simply wishing for change. The ego does not readily dismiss what it holds as your self-awareness; many experiences over the years have reinforced the information stored by your ego. The result is files that are merged and linked to each perception, and until the old information is updated to align with the new information, the ego will default to the original file stored.

The ego, just like a computer, has many safeties built into it to prevent fragmenting a file containing a thought or belief by introducing partial or unsubstantiated information. The ego cannot be rationalized with, dismissed, bypassed, tricked, shut down, or tamed. The ego is simply a data storage system. It is not separate from you and does not have a brain, logic, or judgment. The ego is not an enemy with a battle plan to control you or dictate to you. You provided the information your ego has stored over your lifetime, and unless you replace or update the data, your ego will simply supply what you stored as your awareness of who you are. Even though many of these thoughts no longer serve you, they are what you have available when you call for a reference during an experience. These are the moments and events that blow up on us, the land mines.

As you become more aware of the option to reprogram your ego, it will more frequently challenge you to verify that you want to replace or rewrite data. This is why people often feel they are genetically predisposed to be the way they are. They become aware of a pattern and try to change it, but somehow they keep returning to it. Too often we surrender to the pattern and listen to our ego, feeling we cannot change. How often do we hear words like these? "I can't change." "My father or mother were the same way." "It's how I'm wired." "My family has had these characteristics for generations." "I don't know how." "I can't." "I am afraid of being hurt." "I always lose." "I'm too young." "I'm too old." "It's too late." "I'm too shy." "I tried that before and don't want to do that again." "What's the point?" "There's nothing special about me." "I'm just an average Joe." "Good things happen to other people, not me." "In my family, we have always had to work hard to get ahead." And on and on!

How many of these lines resonate with you? How many can you recite that I did not list? You can see that these thoughts are subtle, often ingrained into our subconscious and often not considered at all. Many of these falsehoods about us are confirmed by friends, family, colleagues, the media, commercials, coaches, doctors, priests, psychologists, psychics, support groups, blogs, websites, and the list goes on. Many of us have accepted these statements about our character as truth for so long ago that we are running on auto pilot, not even aware of the path we are following.

I wish I could tell you that taking charge, correcting the data, and charting your own course are easy things to do. They are not. But the journey is worth taking, and if you undergo this process you will enjoy freedom, security, and peace. Your ego is unique to you, and for some, the programming is not as simple to rewrite and replace as it is for others. This is why I cannot make any promises of success. You are on your own life course and have your own free will, ego, determination, and desires. No one can do this for you. I will share this process and the experiences of myself and others in hopes that this will assist you on your journey. You can have complete success if you are willing to do the work and keep your eye on the goal. The ego will challenge you in many ways and at every step. I welcome this now, since I consider it a sign that I am getting results. Do not let any challenges, roadblocks or surprise turns discourage you. Hold on to this information so that on the days when you feel like you have two left feet, you won't lose your balance. Remember this as your default response to a challenge, a negative thought, a sad or disappointed feeling, and before long you will discover these are temporary events, thoughts, and emotions.

I pride myself in having achieved this awareness, though I learned much of it the hard way. If awards were given for foolish mistakes, categories for "nice try" and "When will you ever learn?," I would have a wall full of them! I have earned a PhD from the school of hard knocks. For many years, my ego held a file reminding me that I was not smart enough to make a decision on my own. That one awareness caused me to second-guess myself and listen to anyone but me. In fact, this negative perception was proven correct many times over. It took some doing for me to reprogram my ego to hold the fact that I am competent at making decisions 99 percent of the time, and the other 1 percent of the time, I can always turn things around. I spent years second-guessing myself! My ego also held the awareness that when I finally made a decision I needed to prepare for the worst-case scenario. Add the law of attraction and I could write a book on how much heartache, headache, and disappointment I suffered and how much time I squandered because of that belief. My ego held on to that perception tenaciously. I faced challenge after challenge before reprogramming that assumption.

I speak from experience when I say the ego will challenge your requests to rewrite files. But doing it was more than worth the work, persistence, and determination. I hope that you do not need to obtain your education in the school of hard knocks and that sharing what I have discovered will shorten the process for you. My only goal is to be an authentic-living coach with the mission to help those looking for more to find it! Many say they do not know what is missing in their lives or what they are looking for. The best news is that learning to dance with your ego will lead you to the answers to these questions. It all begins with the willingness to be your authentic self instead of the self you thought you should be.

I recall the day when I discovered that my ego was keeping me focused on all the negative, limiting stuff in my life. At that moment, I decided not only to listen but to hear the words of my genuine self.

For me, the cloud that overshadowed so much of my life was feeling unworthy and unwanted. I spent many years in shelters, foster care facilities, and with relatives when my parents were not available to care for me and my siblings. Even though our family was known by the police for many domestic violence episodes, I was always sent back to live with my parents. When I ran away or was put out on the streets by my mother, the police would always return me to the violence, to the scary environment into which I was born. At that young age, I concluded that being brought back time and again to parents who did not want me, who told me that I was the problem and that it was my fault they were not happy, was proof that I was not worthy. I decided that if I was worthy, then the police, the people in whose care I was placed, would have fought to keep me safe. I felt unwanted and abandoned by the world. I felt there was no one I could depend on or go to for protection. I was afraid to fall asleep at night, terrified that my parents would fight and that someone would be hurt or killed. I woke up every day happy I was still alive and my siblings and parents were, too. My strategy as a young child was to do whatever I needed to do to keep my parents from fighting so that no one would be harmed, waiting until I was old enough for the police to stop taking me back. I prayed that I would live long enough to get out on my own.

This was what I filed in my ego's database as an innocent little girl, and as I look back, I can see how this information ran through my life like a virus, infecting my decisions, my ability to trust, my willingness to let go, and my judgments, and spawning fear. Just about every vein of my being was affected in one way or another by events more than fifty years earlier.

One day I was sitting at my desk questioning why I could not fill the emptiness that resulted from all the evidence that I was not wanted. Considering the team of friends, colleagues, and family around me, all healthy, balanced relationships, why did I still feel so hollow? Then I recognized that if I listed the attributes describing who I was, I was not useless, unpleasant, untrustworthy, dishonest, or anything else that would make a person unwanted. Still, something was out of whack. I was not a monster, yet it was okay to think I was not lovable, valuable, or desirable! Wow! Where was all this coming from? As I stared out of the window, looking at the pastures of grain, I got it with great clarity. My ego saw me as unwanted, and each time I applied myself toward a different outcome, I defaulted to the ego definition. My ego didn't stop talking to me. It reminded me of the feelings of being hurt, scared, and alone, and before long I was testing people to see if they wanted me. These were unreasonable tests that would make anyone walk away. I saw it all: the ego stepping in and reminding me of the last time, the dos and don'ts, the cautions and the never-ending list of reasons my challenges would only result in more disappointment. A movie seemed to play in my mind. I saw the many times that this one belief that I was not wanted had cost me great opportunities and relationships. I was focused on protecting myself. I did not feel safe in my childhood, so it was easy to see why I developed a need to feel protected and why I could not trust anyone to take care of me.

Fifty years later, I was no longer in an unsafe environment, yet self-doubt continued to dominate my description of who I was. Every moment of every day, my ego reminded me of all the mistakes and disappointments over the years and of how I was the common denominator and therefore not capable of making good decisions. I was convinced that I had to question myself all the time. When I listed the attributes of someone who would be unwanted by society and compared this with the list of my attributes—my genuine self, caring, generous, kind, loving, and courageous—I saw that these lists were polar opposites. At that moment I decided to make a conscious effort to hear the voice of my authentic self, which was being drowned out by the voice of my ego. I realized that I had listened to the voice of my ego for so long that it was the only voice I was hearing. I knew at a logical level that I was not someone who needed to be banished from society, yet I was unknowingly pushing people away, setting myself up for failure and disappointment, since this was the information my ego provided. It has taken a good year since this breakthrough to discover how protected these files of data held by the ego are. They do not change overnight, but the process of making permanent change happen is doable and well worth the work.

Since I embraced my genuine self, paying great attention to my ego awareness, a number of challenges have arisen. My decision to share this revelation by writing this book is a great example. My ego asked who I thought I was to write on such a topic and said I had too many other responsibilities to find time to write a book. Then there was the warning that I did not have the money to publish a book and that no publisher would look at a first-time author. And this was a good one. *If I focus on writing this book, my company will fail!* (After eighteen years?) And here's a great one. *I will add stress to my life, which will add weight when I am working to lose belly fat.*

I will share my experiences as they fit the theme of each chapter so that you will have examples to assist in your process. For now I can only laugh at the irony of being challenged so vehemently by my ego as I choose to take the lead in my life, committed to providing whatever data my ego needs to rewrite the files stored over the past fifty-eight years. I am grateful that I have a sense of humor and the patience to keep on pushing through the fog and mud. It took me from October 2011, when I had the idea to write this book, to June 2012 to get the words flowing on paper. I was reminded daily of why I was foolish to pursue this book idea. Here is a short list of my ego's awareness of who I am. I hope you will see the humor. These lines are so obviously based on fear and denial that even my ego was not able to sell me on this data being the truth. *I am too old, and people will laugh at me for taking so long to "get it." Who am I to think I have anything of value to share? The process worked for me, but will not work for others. If I was truly living authentically, I would be rich and I would not have weight issues.* And there were further doubts. *What credentials do you have? You don't have a doctorate. You have no proof this can work for anyone else.*

These are not words of encouragement but of intimidation and discouragement. This was the partial list of reasons I should not and could not write this book and would fail if I did or if I believed that I was living my life authentically! A bit harsh, would you agree? Amazing to think that these thoughts were running around in my mind! Yes, my ego is alive and well, doing what it is there to do. At least I know my ego is healthy and intact.

These words had a hold on me for a number of months after I first sat down to write this book and share what I had discovered. In March 2012, I lost my voice for ten days. This was the first time I had been sick for more than a day or two in around fifteen years. I could not work, since I could not speak to my clients or staff. I slept a lot, watched TV, and spent many hours feeling beaten and discouraged, telling myself to return to reality and let this book idea go. I meditated and explored why I lost my voice. I concluded that the universe was sending me a message that if I would not speak my truth, then I didn't need a voice. That simple message hit me like a bucket of cold water. I snapped out of the haze in a flash. I again recognized this as the work of my ego and stepped up to the plate and said no more. I now am vigilant in paying attention to whether I am listening to my ego or to my authentic self.

Since that March, events have aligned with ease. My voice returned, I got off the couch, and here I am, sharing what I know. You be the judge. My ego is no longer permitted to act in that capacity. Since I accepted this challenge, the clarity has been exciting, the information emerging is intriguing, and my ego's challenges have become stronger than ever, which affirms that I am changing permanent data. I am excited and welcome the challenges, since this gives me insight on where to focus in reprogramming my ego. It is interesting how quickly a thought becomes a reality. I am manifesting things at an amazing rate.

I am no longer being blindsided; there are no more surprises, doubts, or fears. I have a peace within, knowing that I am willing to give all that I can and that this is enough. What I share will be of value to some and not to others, and that's okay. If this book helps even one person find a way to unleash his genuine self, to take the lead in the dance with his ego, then I will smile, knowing I have paid it forward, offering a gift that was meant to be shared.

Chapter 4

What Is Your Dance Style?

$\mathcal{D}$o you believe in fairy tales? I believe in happy endings, and fairy tales always have happy endings. I believe in the wonderful feelings fairy tales bring to life.

Let's take a look at a few of the classic fairy tales and see if we can relate to these stories.

First, there is Cinderella. Her wicked stepmother and stepsisters show her no respect. They treat her as their servant and control every aspect of her life. She feels trapped like a caged bird. She looks out from behind her bars, longing to fly, to feel free, to make her own choices, to be beautiful, to be wanted, and to be loved. Her family keeps her hidden when Prince Charming searches for a bride. Although she feels ashamed and unworthy of the prince's attention, Cinderella longs to be swept away by him. She dreams of being loved and adored.

Can you relate to Cinderella? Do you feel her pain? Do you understand her anxiety and her longing? The prince rescues her from the evil stepmother and mean stepsisters, and Cinderella lives happily ever after. If this happened in real life, the young woman would need to heal a limiting view of who she is before she could feel confident, beautiful, and worthy of any man's attention. Rescue from a caged environment is often a prelude to recreating that environment. This is evidenced by the people who say they married their mother or their father. This is called repeating the cycle.

The goal is not to be rescued but to be freed from feelings of inadequacy, failure, loneliness, fear, and pain. These feelings are the bars on the cage that hold us back, just as they trapped Cinderella. Feelings of unworthiness and insecurity keep us from stepping out of our comfort zone and believing in our dreams of living happily ever after. We all want to be Cinderella or Prince Charming and live happily ever after. No one dreams of being controlled and neglected! Cinderella's ego filed her personal perception information based on what she was told and how she was treated by her stepmother and stepsisters while growing up. Though Cinderella had become a woman and a contender in Prince Charming's search for a wife, she continued to see herself as the awareness held by her ego, which told her that she did not deserve to be his bride.

Cinderella tried to step out by making a new dress, but facing attacks from unsupportive family members, she fell back into the same pattern of unworthiness. When she longed to be with the prince and wanted to leave her comfort zone, her ego brought forward the information that she had stored, reminding her that she was not qualified to be his wife. With this information, which her rational mind supported with feelings of fear and anxiety, Cinderella did not believe she had a chance to live her dream. But after she encountered the fairy godmother, Cinderella found her next attempt to break free much easier. Still, it was easy for her to slide back into her old ways after the ball. She returned home to her old life. She was unable to permanently reprogram her ego until, taking courage in hand, she put her best foot forward and tried on the shoe.

We don't know if Cinderella and Prince Charming indeed lived happily ever after, because the story ends when he finds her again. However, we are led to believe they did.

In real life, we know that we develop patterns and habits and repeat cycles and that we often sabotage ourselves when things seem to be too good to be true. We never stop wanting life to be different. We battle frustration and discouragement when we put great effort into making change happen and then find ourselves right back where we started. Our ego again reminds us of our limits, but soon we find ourselves moving on despite these messages. Too many times, however, we do so with less enthusiasm and weakened willpower, reminded that we might not be good enough to succeed. Then family and friends, worried that we are expecting too much of ourselves, may tell us, "Get real." They say this with great concern for our well-being, hoping we will stop wanting more than what we have, and yet the words "Get real" encourage us to find our true self amid all the confusion.

Focus on the authentic you hidden beyond the ego's awareness. There is more to you than the eye can see. Go within and see what you find when you are willing to accept who you are and how you want to live. You just might find yourself living happily ever after!

Now let's take a look at Snow White and the seven dwarfs. Snow White, a beautiful, vibrant woman with a kind heart and the patience of an angel, is resented and despised by her stepmother, the evil queen. The queen is jealous of Snow White and fears that she may be the fairest in the land. The queen orders Snow White's death.

The servant tasked with returning Snow White's heart to the queen is unable to kill the princess and tells her of the queen's order, insisting that she run away and never return. As Snow White runs, the trees turn into monsters and leaves angrily chase her until she falls asleep amid the spinning craziness. She is awakened by birds singing and deer, rabbits, and raccoons playing, and notices them watching her. Snow White realizes the forest is not her enemy. It was her fear as she ran that made the forest appear dangerous. She explains her problem to the animals and birds and they guide her to the home of the seven dwarfs. The queen learns Snow White is still alive and uses her black magic to secure her position as the fairest in the land. She creates a potion that changes her into an old hag. Then she drops by the dwarfs' cottage and convinces Snow White to eat an apple poisoned with a magic death spell. The only thing that can wake Snow White is the kiss of her perfect love. The prince arrives, kisses Snow White, and they ride off into the sunset to live happily ever after.

Another happy ending, with a rescue by a valiant, perfect hero of a man. I often ponder what this image does to the expectations of men and women trying to sustain relationships. Does the man now need to rescue the woman every day? Once a month? When will she be capable of doing things herself without having to assure him that he is still her hero?

These fairy tales contain so many dynamics that we could easily get sidetracked. Let's focus on the information stored in Snow White's ego. Does she fear the queen? Is she ashamed because her beauty is so great that the queen feels threatened? Does she feel it is safer to hide and become invisible? Is she diminishing who she is to please the queen? Is Snow White fully confident in what she knows to be true, that her stepmother, the wicked queen, is capable of killing her? With this knowledge,

Snow White moves on, planning to take care of herself, without assigning blame or feeling pity. She comes across the home of the seven dwarfs and offers to cook and clean in exchange for a place to live as she hides from the queen. She is not waiting to be rescued by a dashing prince. Instead, Snow White sings, "One day my prince will come," knowing they will meet, and she enjoys every day, dancing and singing with her new friends.

Have you ever felt you can be happy no matter what life throws at you? If so, you have something in common with Snow White. It would have been easy for Snow White to store fear and shame in her ego's files, and she would have been justified, considering that her stepmother was jealous enough to want her dead. Snow White felt she needed to hide for her safety. But she was not hiding because of fear. What if her ego stored that information and Snow White became shy and afraid to speak her truth? Snow White was not a woman needing rescue. Instead, she was put under a spell that could be broken only by her true love's kiss. Snow White's strength in never doubting that her prince would come is a model for all of us to follow. I love this story because it shows Snow White as a strong woman who loved nature and faced challenges without fear. Fear takes hold of her for a short time, but she realizes that fear itself is creating a scary experience. She moves forward, choosing to be trusting and loving and knowing that life is wonderful. Snow White's happy ending demonstrates the power of knowing and believing with conviction.

Compare your ego's information to Snow White's. Are you getting the positive feedback that she did? You know that you care about and respect the people around you and that you do not need to be smaller, dimmer, quieter, hidden, or invisible. If you recognize this but still behave in a diminished way most of the time, it is because your ego has not received updated information about you. Is your ego interfering when you want to shine, be bold, and speak your truth? You don't need a prince to kiss you to break the spell. You have the power to break this spell by taking charge of the information your ego has stored and will provide when you draw on an awareness of who you are.

Now let's explore Beauty and the Beast, another classic starring a beautiful woman. The difference in this story is that Belle, our leading lady, is considered odd by the townsfolk because she loves to read, dreams of adventure, and is not dazzled by Gaston, the town hunk and dream catch. Belle gets her wish and has the adventure of her dreams. She finds herself sentenced to life within the walls of a castle ruled by the Beast. He is really a prince punished for being self-centered and heartless. A spell turned him into a beast and transformed his servants and staff into furniture and fixtures in the castle. The Beast can be returned to human form only if he falls in love and is loved in return. This must happen before the last petal on a rose falls.

Belle, not the shy type, is curious about the secret lair in the west wing that the Beast has banned her from entering. The Beast has created a space where the mirrors are broken and there is no color or pleasure. He has given up hope, is unkind and impatient, and is angry at anyone who dares enter his home. His temper gets the better of him most days as he chooses to hide and remain in his lair. He is convinced that with his beastly appearance he is unworthy of anyone's company, especially that of a beautiful woman. Belle escapes to find her father and instead is surrounded by wolves. The Beast comes to her rescue and a friendship begins. The Beast falls in love with Belle and sets her free, since she longs to find her father. By letting her go, the Beast sacrifices the possibility of being returned to human form. His love for her will not allow him to hold her when she is not happy. The townspeople learn of the Beast, decide he must be destroyed, and attack the castle. Gaston, the town hunk, determined to show off his manhood, leads the pack, vowing to kill the Beast and to marry Belle. Belle rescues the Beast, who is injured. As he is dying, she professes her love for him just as the last petal falls. The Beast returns to his princely form, the servants return to their prior selves, and they all live happily ever after.

So our leading lady is not looking to be saved like Cinderella or dreaming of her prince to come like Snow White. Belle is ridiculed by the townspeople, who think she is odd because she dares to learn and dream. Circumstances lead her to the castle and ultimately her prince, However, they rescue each other before living happily ever after. She sees her prince for the man he is, not as a solution to her limited existence. He views himself as a beast and is feared by the townspeople, who simply react to his appearance and never think for themselves. Our ego stores data based on the information we obtain from the masses and hold as truths. Are you a Belle, a Beast, or one of the townspeople? Identifying which of these characters most describes you will give you valuable insight into the information your ego has stored on your behalf.

The story of Dumbo was my favorite tale when I was a child. I could relate to him, not because my ears were too big, but because I felt that I never fit in. My family moved constantly and so I frequently changed schools, at times more than once a year. I was scrawny, wore glasses, had ringlets in my hair, and big teeth, and I stuttered. I saw myself as the ugly duckling, because that's what I was told almost daily. Add to this that I was shy. I wanted to blend into the wallpaper and was terrified that someone would notice me and ask me to speak. I was teased and laughed at and lived in fear that my parents would find out, because I knew that I would be punished for causing them more stress. I was to be a good girl and keep quiet.

I was equally afraid that the schools would learn of my home life and interfere by talking to my parents or the authorities, for which I would again be punished. So I understood how Dumbo felt with no friends and no mother, once she was taken from him. No one cared about how Dumbo felt, and I understood how empty and frightening that was. As I got older, I was constantly selected to be the captain of teams and the leader of groups and soon found I excelled at many things. The difference was that everyone cheered when Dumbo discovered he could fly, but I was punished when I took home awards. I was told I was being selfish and expecting to be treated like I was better than my siblings.

In my late teens I met a man who became my Timothy Q. Mouse. He was in my life for only a short time but he sparked a flame in me, reminding me of the courage of little Dumbo. He didn't let me hide inside myself, and he taught me to dare to dream. The older I got, the more I came to love and be grateful for the lesson Dumbo taught me: You can live by the limitations of your challenges or you can focus on the opportunities around you. I think of that little elephant with the big ears when I feel overwhelmed, and send a quiet thank-you to my personal Timothy Q. Mouse. My life has paralleled Dumbo's in many ways. I am a public speaker, admired by many. No longer shy and introverted or afraid of my own shadow, I love my life and the joys and the challenges equally. I no longer feel I need to hide or be quiet. I speak what I believe is the truth and don't worry about what others think of me; it is none of my business. I look to my internal self, the me at the center of my being, the me that walks in my shoes, and I will not be influenced by anything that does not serve my desire to share, care, and love fully. When I look in the mirror, I want to feel proud of who I am, what I do, and why I do it. It is that simple. Dumbo and I found our hidden talents as we let ourselves be visible, and the world embraced us—a happy ending for both of us. I discovered I didn't need big ears to fly, just faith, trust, and a lot of love!

I love fairy tales because they are filled with messages and insights. It is critically important to think about who you would like to be and to examine how far you might be from this goal. The self you are experiencing is the self led by your ego's perception of who you are, based on the information stored. If you long for a different life at any level, you must do what it takes to change the data stored by your ego into that awareness. Choose who you want to be and then do the work to reprogram your ego. Update your consciousness so that going forward your ego and your genuine self are going in the direction you choose. Take charge of choosing your dance style. Are you someone who wants to live an adventurous life like Belle, or are you hoping to be rescued like Cinderella? Maybe you are Snow White, confident, loving, kind, and generous, but instead of trusting that you can be loved as she did, you feel you need someone to verify that you are okay, giving you that stamp of approval before you can feel safe expressing your genuine self.

Whether you are aware of your style or not, you do have one. You could be running so fast that you can't hear the music. Your style could be slow, steady, and cozy; it could be a formal ballroom style or possibly a fast, free style. But don't sit on the sidelines waiting for someone to drag you onto the dance floor. This is your life. Your time here is short. Get into the dance, let your music out, and let yourself be heard. There is a style that is not only right for you, but that is uniquely yours, and when you get into step with it, you will flow freely and joyously in all aspects of your life. Find your style, embrace what feels right, and live the happy ending of your life's fairy tale.

Remember what I learned from Timothy Q. Mouse: you can live by the limitations of your challenges or you can focus on the opportunities around you.

> *Argue for your limitations and,*
> *sure enough, they're yours.*

—Richard Bach, *Illusions*

Chapter 5

~~~~~~~~

Do You Matter?

Make the most of yourself, for
that is all there is of you.

—Ralph Waldo Emerson

*D*o you matter? To whom do you matter and why is it important to matter? I have listened to hundreds, maybe even thousands, of inspirational people, from those with PhDs to those who are homeless and living with addictions. They have one thing in common: they all say that when they die they want to know they mattered.

When will you know that you matter? This question is universal. Who or what is going to give you the stamp of achievement to verify that you matter? This desire is very different from wanting to make a difference or to leave a legacy. These are important goals to many, but countless people simply want to know that they matter.

Is this the same void within our core being that says we are not wanted, smart enough, good enough, valued, or worthy? When did we decide it was important to matter? Was it as an infant, a toddler, a child, a teen, a young adult, or an adult? An infant has one focus, making sure that basic needs like being fed, being cared for, and remaining safe are met. A toddler explores his environment with a little more intention; toddlers operate from trust until they have an experience that is not warm, safe, and caring. Children push buttons, trying to see what works and what does not. They feel invincible but are very aware of the expectations of others, what feels good, and what causes pain. With hormonal changes sending confusing messages, the average teenager is not concerned about whether he matters.

After a near-death experience, many adults say not having the answer to this question inspires them to take charge of their lives. Most adults seem to contemplate the question as they get older and as they complete goals and experience success. In any case, this seems to be a dominant question for many people over thirty. That's a lot of people!

So where do we begin to look for the answer? Do we look to psychology, spirituality, religion, education, our guru, our parents and grandparents? The only correct answer is to go within, access your inner self, and ask if you matter.

There is only one answer: yes.

Every human being matters. Each of us contributes to the daily experiences of this planet. Even after we die, people who love us, who like us, or who know us keep our spirit alive, allowing us to continue to matter. If you don't believe this, think of Elvis Presley, Marilyn Monroe, John F. Kennedy, or your favorite aunt, uncle, or grandparent. Consider how many people are spoken of and remembered for generations after they have passed on. Does this not prove that they mattered? This applies to babies, puppies, pets, loved ones, and celebrities. No one is exempt from adding to this world!

Now that you know you matter, the more important question is, why do so many people feel that they do not matter? Is this true for you? It was a question I asked myself for most of my life. I understood that we are all part of life's grand tapestry, and I knew that even insignificant little me counted for something, but knowing this did not fill the void that I felt deep inside. I wanted to know what about me mattered. Did I make a difference, and if yes, then to whom? Why did this void leave me feeling lost, out of sorts, confused, unsatisfied, and believing I needed to find something or someone? I had no idea what would satisfy this emptiness inside, but I knew I needed to keep looking until I found it. This search took many years and many forms, including failed careers, failed relationships, poor food choices, and poor health as well as successes, insights, and inspiration from many sources. The void is now filled with joy, love, magic, and peace.

I learned in this search that the answer to the question "Do I matter?" is actually my "why." The why in our lives is what motivates us. When we have no why, we drift, feel empty, uninterested, lost, and disconnected. We must identify our why before we can achieve our goal. To be motivated to achieve a goal, we need to know why it is of value. Answering why we are driven to care about something enough to give it our energy and attention makes our actions matter. Knowing that we matter motivates us to strive to be our best selves, a key component to living an authentic life.

As I tried to learn who I was and if I mattered, I was physically collapsing as my body responded to the pain, fear, and confusion I held quietly within for so many years. At thirty, I was on three inhalers, antidepressant drugs, and antihistamines and I was regularly in hospitals or clinics for heart monitoring or to deal with asthma attacks. I could barely function for four hours at a time. This was particularly stressful, since I was a single parent and needed to support my family. I was diagnosed with cancer at thirty-one and again at forty-two. At my unhealthiest point, I tested positive for 114 environmental allergies and 225 food allergies, the maximum doctors could test for. At twenty-eight, I was told that I would need an oxygen tank by the time I was forty. My weight ballooned in my early thirties and I could not take it off, no matter what I tried, and I tried everything. I felt that my body was attacking me. I couldn't do even simple things like eat, breathe, or drink chlorinated water, basics of living. I felt completely undeserving and rejected by life. This was evident as my body rejected life's simple needs.

Today, I am fifty-eight and have not had an asthma attack since 1995. I have not taken any prescription or over-the-counter medications since 1998. I have not had the flu or a cold lasting more than a few hours for more than fifteen years (with the exception of losing my voice in the spring of 2012). My weight began to come off when I started respecting and listening to my genuine self.

So how did I go from being unable to function to super healthy, energized, and happy? The answer is simple. I took back the lead role in my life and cleaned up the programming that my ego draws from. I still find the odd bit of data not to my liking, but it takes only a moment to correct this and update the information. The freedom, the security, the awe of it all are what I want you to have.

The next chapters will walk you through the steps I took to claim the lead role in my life. I have provided exercises you can do in the privacy of your home to achieve success.

I hope that these exercises will lead you to take charge of your life, to let your genuine self be visible and heard. You can change the programming that is limiting you and encourage and enhance yourself. The answers are within you, waiting for you to embrace them. You will see results if you stick to the goal. As with any project or challenge, you must participate, practice, and go the distance. There are no shortcuts. We all must make our own journey. I hope that you will gain insight from the tips and stories shared on these pages and that they will make your journey shorter than mine. Maybe there will even be some fun along the way.

A word of caution: as you move from your ego self to your genuine self, many friends, colleagues, and even family members may not like the changes that occur in you. They could challenge and warn you and express worry, and this could create confusion, doubt, fear, and a sense of your loyalty being questioned. Be aware of this possibility and be prepared in case this is what you experience. Have a plan for how you will deal with this. You might explain to family members or friends that you are doing personal development work. Be clear that you need them to support you during this process. Ask them to listen and not give advice or ask them to remind you why you are doing this when you feel discouraged. Ask them if they can do this for you on your terms. If they are not able or willing to support you in the way you need, thank them for their honesty and politely and respectfully let them know you will not be sharing this journey with them. It is important to surround yourself with people who support your determination to live as your authentic self. One concrete step you can take is to be clear in your own mind about who in your life supports you and who does not.

Being surrounded by people willing to support you will honor your desire to matter and help reinforce your intent. This will also assist you in reprogramming your ego. The ego will side with all those who are concerned about you and sincerely want to protect you for your own good because they love you.

The ego can be quite strong and convincing when it is not in alignment with your actions. The people in your life know you as the person that your ego's awareness presents you as being today. People by nature do not like change, especially when that change affects a close relationship. The stronger the challenge, the closer you are to achieving success. It took losing my voice and being unable to work or speak for me to stop and listen to my authentic voice. That voice was being drowned out by my ego's determination to hold on to the old programming. That is how strong and how loud your ego can be. Be prepared. I am with you at each step. Trust that your genuine self will not lead you into harm or embarrassment. It is your ego that stands between you living the life you long for and the one you are experiencing.

Chapter 6

AM I WHO I WANT TO BE?

It took me a long time not to judge
myself through someone else's eyes.

—Sally Field

efine success. What does it mean to you? When will you know you have achieved success? To answer these questions, we first need to know who we want to be. If we achieve success but it is not in alignment with our genuine self, we will continue to feel unsatisfied and disappointed or sense something missing. Real joy and celebration come from feeling a connection within that honors who we truly are.

In this first exercise, I want you set up a special place in your home where you can think, reflect, meditate, or pray. This should be your private space where you can surround yourself with your favorite things. These might include pictures, scents, flowers, books, teddy bears— whatever gives you joy, peace, and calm. This space should be a place that others, including children and partners, enter only with your permission. Ask family members to respect this space and invite them to create their own sanctuaries.

I have a room in my basement that has a window for natural light. I painted it lavender; it has bookshelves, a rocking chair, and a writing desk covered with a lace tablecloth, pictures of my family, and many candles. No work-related books or projects are allowed in this room, and few people have entered this space. It is adorned with colors, scents, and pictures of angels, fairies, palm trees, and sunsets. Favorite sayings and quotes cover the walls, as do my dream boards, which I regularly update. You will find over time that as this space takes shape, it becomes a place of rejuvenation after a hectic day, of centering when you feel out of balance. My space is healing and loving. I feel safe, reminded of all the greatness in the world and in me. It is a gift to be able to sit in this room created with the things I love and feel its calming energy.

One night there were tornado warnings for our area, and I entered the basement to seek shelter. I took my two dogs, a can of sardines, a bag of mixed nuts, water, and a lantern into this space to wait out the storm, and surprisingly felt no anxiety. I listened to the eerie stillness as I sat in the eye of the storm. No leaves rustled, no birds chirped; there was no sound from horses running, no thunder or wind, just quiet, as if time were standing still. This stillness lasted ten minutes, and instead of feeling fear, I felt joy at being able to observe it. A wave of hail, rain, and wind passed in only a few moments, but the memory of feeling safe in the eye of a storm will stay with me forever. If I had been in any other area of my home, I would not have experienced this calm. I credit this to the sanctuary I created.

If you do not have a room or space that can be sustained as

your sanctuary, collect your favorite things and surround yourself with them when you meditate, soak in the tub, or simply take time to relax. I began doing this twenty years ago, surrounding my bathtub with candles, playing soft, soothing music, and filling the tub with bubbles and scents. This was the only space where I was not interrupted, so I claimed it several times a week. I would read, meditate, or listen to music and relax. Doing this was the first step to taking back my life, to finding out who I truly was and who I wanted to be. I did not know then that such a small and enjoyable exercise would change my life forever.

Once you have established your sanctuary and feel the desire to spend time in this place, you will be ready to move to the next step.

Exercise Two

As you settle into your sanctuary, make a list of your attributes. Preface each with the words "I am." (I am honest; I am kind; I am generous; I am courageous; I am confident.)

List at least ten qualities that speak to who you are. Start with negative attributes and then list ten positive attributes. We all have both, and part of being aware is to recognize both. Notice how you feel about doing this exercise. Was it difficult or easy to complete these lists? Was it easier to list your negative attributes? If so, you should be aware that this often is the case, so you are not alone. Note that these are the attributes your ego is holding in your awareness now.

When you have completed this process, provide at least ten responses to complete this sentence.

"I want to be _____

_____ ."

To answer this question, take time to reflect. Go back to your childhood dreams, and remember your plans and expectations for being an adult. The answers should represent your ideal self if you had no obstacles, no challenges, no missed opportunities—in other words, if you lived in a perfect world where you could do whatever you wanted. This may seems silly, but it won't hurt. These are words written only for your eyes. Once you are done, compare the answers. Are there differences between who you are and who you want to be?

When I did this exercise back in 1995, I found it difficult to define who I wanted to be. Pretending there were no obstacles, I found there were too many choices. I had no idea where to begin. If I could relive my life, what would I do? When I did this exercise, I cleared the slate and approached the question assuming I could do anything. It was interesting to see how big the challenge was. I am glad that I stuck with it and did the exercise with such an open mind. After using reams of paper and producing list after list, I realized that who I wanted to be had nothing to do with a career, making money, being married or single, having children, a big house on a hill, or high fashion in my closet. I was not defined by where I lived or any of the things I had listed as goals. After much deliberation on the question, I learned that I could not be defined by things.

With this awareness, I decided to define who I wanted to be in a broader way. I started with a blank piece of flip chart paper, about twenty-four by twenty-eight inches. I picked my favorite colored flip chart markers and set out to solve this puzzle. I started by writing "My Dream" in the center and framed these words with a cloud. From this point, several statements flowed: I wanted to make a difference in the world, I wanted to travel, I wanted loving relationships, I wanted freedom of choice, I wanted money and a good lifestyle, and I wanted to add something to this world. Seeing these words in front of me on paper, I realized that if I attained all of these goals, I would have an amazing life and I would be proud to be me. From there, I decided to identify the characteristics a person would need to achieve these six goals. As I look back seventeen years later, these things have all come to be who I am. This is what I wrote.

1. Statement: I want to make a difference in this world.

   a. Characteristics: participate, take chances, be independent, have courage

2. Statement: I want to travel.

   a. Characteristics: need time, money, and a destination

3. Statement: I want loving relationships.

   a. Characteristics: give 100 percent of your genuine self, acceptance, and commitment

4. Statement: I want freedom of choice.

   a. Characteristics: money, mindfulness, great health

5. Statement: I want money and a good lifestyle.

   a. Characteristics: express 100 percent from trust, gratitude, and love, and be creative

6. Statement: I want to add something to this world.

   a. Characteristics: honesty and acceptance of difference

I framed these words and have had them on my wall ever since. I have the life I live today thanks to the time I spent finding these qualities deep within myself. People often tell me I am lucky and I agree, but I know that luck took me close to twenty years to create. It all started with the simple process of searching my heart and soul, letting go of the limitations my ego held for me, and putting these statements about who I wanted to be in writing for my eyes to see, my heart to feel, and my spirit to embrace.

When I completed this visual board in 1995, my only travel had been from Calgary west to Vancouver and east to Saskatoon. I had never been to Edmonton three hours north. I was struggling with my health and living with a kind friend who provided a foam mat on the floor in a room I shared with her niece. I had lost everything the year before and was just beginning to rebuild my life. In 1997, less than two years later, I was regularly traveling to Chicago, Toronto, and throughout the Caribbean and Mexico for business. My health improved and my life started coming together again.

I will share experiences with you as they become relevant to the process of finding your genuine self. I remain grateful for the valuable experience I obtained on this journey. I found each step by hitting a wall, losing an opportunity, running out of money or time, or having poor health. With each of these experiences, I found the path to correct the process. Finally, although there is much more to experience and my journey is far from over, I am thrilled to say I love who I am, I am proud of my success, and I feel confident and solid instead of shaky and doubtful. I write this in 2012, seventeen years after I defined who I wanted to be. Today when I am asked to define success, this is how I respond. Three tips for achieving a successful life are: 1) know who you want to be, 2) know your authentic self, and 3) commit to living life fully.

I have come to appreciate that by applying these three tips we can achieve any goal whether personal and professional. Getting to know myself, the good, the bad, and the ugly, took determination, commitment, and perseverance. Thanks to the generosity of a friend, I was able to begin again. I started a new company and became even more determined to keep going. The first year's sales were $5,000, which I used to leverage more sales, thanks to this friend's kindness.

This time as I started over, I was determined not to recreate the failed pattern. To avoid this, I listened, observed, and questioned my thoughts, actions, and outcomes.

Having spent much of my childhood living in abandoned buildings, shelters, and with relatives, I realized that being homeless and hungry was a familiar experience for me. I read every book I could find about breaking the cycles and why this was so hard to do.

I was so grateful to anyone who was kind or helpful that I overdid the gratitude. I spent a lot of money and energy, thinking I was helping people who had been good to me, in addition to spending money and time trying to save family members. I wanted to give back. I did not realize that I had not developed healthy boundaries and habits for taking care of myself. These are essential before we can provide valuable service to others. (Recall the oxygen mask example.) As a result of not being in healthy balance, I was taken advantage of many times over the years. Giving back is a good thing, but there must be a fair exchange, which will result from healthy balance and boundaries.

As you evolve and grow into your authentic self, you will discover habits, issues, and parts of yourself that you didn't know existed. As you become healthier and stronger, you will look back in amazement and wonder at how you could have been so naive, foolish, or gullible. Don't be too hard on yourself. You can act only with what you know. See these perceptions for what they are, lessons and information of which you were unaware until now.

Our goal is to expand what you know about who you are, beyond the limits of your ego. There will be moments that require you to look back over your life and laugh at yourself. I often have found myself rolling on the floor, wrapped in a big belly laugh, when I realized how stuck I was in a habit so out of line with my genuine self. At times, it is hard to believe that my ego held these things as my reality.

This journey is one of new discoveries, feelings, thoughts, beliefs, and awareness about who you are. To discover the most in the shortest time, consider yourself to be in a big learning zone. This zone is beyond your horizons; it is that big. Anything you discover is yours to keep, throw away, question, laugh at, or embrace. There are no expectations, guidelines, judgments, or time lines in this learning zone.

So let loose, have fun, make some noise, shine, try new things, keep what you like, and get rid of what you do not want to keep. You have the final say, because it is your life. You are who you want to be in this learning zone. You can choose the limits you live by today or you can choose the opportunities of tomorrow. It is up to you!

Chapter 7

WHY AM I HERE?

I am convinced all of humanity is born with
more gifts than we know. Most are born
geniuses and just get de-geniused rapidly.

—Buckminster Fuller

*Y*ou have now obtained insight into who you are and who you want to be. But are you where you are supposed to be in your life? Are you living with purpose? Are you living your best life? Posing these questions signifies that life has value. Thousands of books, e-books, blogs, coaches, doctors, and gurus tell us that a life without purpose is not really lived. Can all these experts be wrong?

We are born and go in our own unique directions based on our life experiences. Some people are sensitive; others seem heartless. There are those who are frightened and those who are secure. There are multitudes of cultures, beliefs, and practices in communities, and within each community there are subcultures, minicultures, and macrocultures. People have a common desire for peace. Does this peace mean safety and quiet? Does it include peace of mind with no worries? It is interesting that when there is a disaster, whether affecting a single family or an entire city or country, people come together to help. Why? Because it feels good to help someone! Aretha Franklin once said, "When you're feeling blue, don't give up. Just give." I have never forgotten those words. We feel better when we help someone. I have often wondered whether we would see miraculous recoveries if people feeling anxious or depressed were prescribed a community's help instead of drugs.

Are giving, caring, creating, and desiring peace tied to our purpose? This is a big question. How does one begin to find the answer? Time is marching on. We need to get on purpose soon or it will be too late. Does any of this sound familiar? These thoughts drove me for many years as I questioned if I was living my life with purpose and if so, what that purpose was. I don't have any verified talents. I am not a musician or an actor. I am not a guru or a certified teacher. I have little formal education, yet I feel confident in what I have learned even though it was through reading and attending seminars on many topics. I have reached the top in my profession and that feels great, but I do not feel my profession is my purpose. Is writing this book my purpose? No, I don't think it is. I wanted to share what I have discovered, in hopes that others will not need to spend a lifetime overcoming their history, their fears, or the information their egos have stored. Is training horses and dogs my purpose? No, but I love doing these things.

As I list my many activities—writing books, authoring and presenting seminars, traveling, playing drums, coaching others, volunteering, starting companies, serving on committees—I realize that I have done all these things because I care, I want to make a difference, and I am generous with my time and my money. That is who I am. I live with passion because I give all of myself to my life. Have I found my purpose? I have no idea, and it really does not matter, since I am having too much fun to care whether what I do is my purpose. As long as whatever I do is aligned with my authentic self, I am doing want I was born to do, and that's my only purpose. If the great universe has an expectation of me, then it had best give me a bigger sign because I am not seeing one.

I spent many years trying to answer this question because I thought it needed to be answered before I could get the grand seal of approval as a fully actualized person. I read books and attended seminars and programs on how to be the best you can be, how to have great health, and how to have great wealth. I did all the homework and assignments. I followed each program as if my life depended on it. To me, it did. I did not like feeling alone, scared, not smart enough, insecure, unworthy, or undesirable. I was determined to study those who had lots of money, great relationships, stature, confidence, happy families, and great careers and figure out how they achieved these lifestyles.

During the seventeen years I spent attempting to define who I was, I gained weight, had an employee sabotage my business, rebuilt the business just in time for the economy to tank, was sued by people I tried to help, fell in love, had a second marriage end, made money, lost money, family, and friends. I also traveled extensively in the Caribbean and Mexico and fell in love with Hawaii. I wrote a book that sold three thousand copies and is still selling as an e-book. I was recognized as one of Alberta's Women of Vision by the Global TV Network and the YWCA. I became a sought-after speaker highly respected as an expert in my profession. I am admired by many and despised by some. All in all, this is a life many would love to have. Oddly enough, though, I have never been able to answer the questions "Why am I here?" and "What is my purpose?" It seemed to me that people living their passion and working with purpose were extremely wealthy, physically fit, and happy in every area of their lives.

Since I was far from extremely wealthy, was overweight and single, and many people I once considered close friends wanted nothing to do with me, I was sure I had not found my purpose. I was convinced that when I found my calling in life, I would see magical results. All these goals are a smoke screen to keep our egos happy. My ego was constantly pointing out all the items on my list as evidence that I was not living my purpose. The more I listened to my ego, the harder I searched, the more stress I suffered, and the sadder I felt, because I could not figure out my purpose.

On the day when I sat staring out of the window, questioning why I had never been wanted, I assumed this was the reason I didn't have a purpose. At this bottom-of-the-barrel moment, I suddenly got it. This was what my ego thought of me. I became acutely aware that my ego was still running programs from when I was six and scared, ten and shy, fifteen and hopeful, twenty and intimidated by life. To my ego, I was a confused, frightened, and lost person. But the truth was clear. I was not useless, undeserving, undesirable, or worthless. I was not frightened, confused, or lost. I was strong, vibrant, and courageous. I had conquered many fears and achieved many successes, so why would my ego send thoughts that encouraged me to hold on to old beliefs?

I had a schedule filled with people grateful for just five minutes of my time. I had great friends, great staff, and great relationships. I now had healthy boundaries and was no longer giving away my time, my money, or my possessions. I had enough money to live comfortably on my little ranch with my horses, dogs, and cats. I realized at that moment that I did not want for anything and that I could live my way. My ego was holding me hostage to the thought that I needed a clearly defined purpose to validate my life. I decided that I would not entertain those thoughts ever again, and that has been that. Since that moment, I have had no desire to find my purpose. I have concluded that my purpose is to be the best me I can be, to live from my personal truth as my genuine self. I am careful not to buy into propaganda that does not make me feel healthy, beautiful, and wise. With this resolve, the weight has been falling off, my finances have become stabler, and my relationships incredible.

Exercise Three

1. Identify how much time you spend searching for your purpose and your passion.

2. Ask yourself if you are undertaking this search to learn something you really want to know or something you feel you should know.

3. Make a list of at least ten things you love to do.

4. Do one of these things at least three times each week, and give these activities your full attention while doing them.

5. Track an activity for a minimum of three months and record what you did and how you felt during and after. If you felt good, continue doing it. If an activity brought you stress, anxiety, or frustration, do something else for three months, again tracking your feelings. Continue this process for all items on your list.

6. Incorporate into your life on a consistent basis those activities that brought you joy or a sense of well-being.

This exercise will help you identify the things you are passionate about and connect you to them. When an activity makes you feel excited, calm, peaceful, proud, loving, big-hearted, thrilled, happy, strong, light, invincible, courageous, or so pleased you want to shout from a rooftop, you have found your passion. Watch for things that you do in everyday life that produce any of these feelings. It could be walking the dog, admiring a room you just cleaned, jogging on a beach, or fixing a fence. It could be completing a project or achieving a major goal.

Whatever it is, make note and strive to incorporate activities that make you feel good into each day. Start with three times each week for ninety days; then increase the frequency to four days a week, five, six, and seven. You will agree that life is pretty grand when your week is filled with things you love to do.

When you have one of those days that I call "sideways days," when things don't go as you would like, return to your list and remember that tomorrow is another day. (I use the term *sideways days* because I believe there are no bad days. Each day's experience brings more information about who I am and how I am doing, so every day is a blessing. Sideways days are those unexpected days when the best-made plans come to nothing.)

> *Finish each day and be done with it. You have done what you could; some blunders and absurdities have crept in; forget them as soon as you can. Tomorrow is a new day; you shall begin it serenely and with too high a spirit to be encumbered with your old nonsense.*
> —Ralph Waldo Emerson

Enjoy the process, be mindful that it is a process, and remember that this is your private list, not an inventory of things your parents, teacher, partner, or boss wants you to do. You can add items to your list or delete things that you thought you would enjoy but discovered you don't. It is your list to do with as you want whenever you like. You can share your list with others or keep it to yourself. Make it work for you. Share your list only with those who have agreed to be supportive as you venture through this process.

Your purpose is simply to be the best you that you can be. This is the purpose we all have. Some of us are good at speaking, others at being quiet and listening. Some are great at growing flowers, and some at preparing food. Our communities are filled with doctors, lawyers, teachers, students, pilots, politicians, Realtors, buyers, sellers, janitors, bellboys, lobbyists, parents, grandparents, and children. We all have a purpose. No two of us are alike, so we don't need to worry about whether our purpose is unique or of value. We all contribute something. Even grandma who bakes an apple pie on Sunday so we can feel loved is filling a purpose that no one else can fill. So give 100 percent of who you are to all that you do, and you will find your passion. Then relax and enjoy each day as if it were made just for you. It is!

Chapter 8

~~~

YOUR GENUINE SELF OR YOUR EGO SELF?

No one can make you feel inferior
without your consent.

—Eleanor Roosevelt

*N*ow that you are aware that your purpose is to be who you genuinely are, without the limitations portrayed by your ego, another question arises: how do you know if you are living as your authentic self? The question is not as difficult to answer as one might think.

Have you ever followed the rules and done everything right but failed to get the results you expected? Did you feel confused, sad, frustrated, out of your element, foolish, or incapable? Were the majority of your feelings discouraging and negative or were they supportive and positive?

Being aware of your feelings will enable you to choose the

experiences you prefer based on those reactions. In my early days of sorting through feelings and searching for who I wanted to be, I would say, "If it hurts, stop doing it; if it feels good, do it more." At the time, I had no idea how wise those words were and what a powerful filtering system they would prove to be. I thought I was being funny, which was often my way of coping with confusion. I am referring to emotional pain, guilt, anxiety, and fear when I speak of what hurts and to joy, calm, pride, and love when I speak of what feels good. I am not encouraging you to jump off of a cliff or to deny that your guilt, fear, and pain are real. When it comes to determining whether you are expressing your genuine self or your limited ego, the true measure is your feelings and thoughts. If you are giving all that you have but feel like you are swimming upstream and not connecting, it is possible that you are not in alignment with your authentic self. When you are present as your genuine self, the anxiety and the void disappear. When you are genuinely present, everything you do, grand or small, flows. As you change, identifying the old ego programming becomes easier because feeling blue seems out of character for you. When you express yourself from your genuine core, you experience a wonderful way of living. A successful life means having peace, joy, security, and pride in yourself.

This does not mean that every success we have verifies that we are in line with our authentic self. Many people have lives that appear successful by the standards of the propaganda that our ego has stored in our data bank. But if you are not happy or at peace with your achievements, you should evaluate your definition of success and ask if it is in line with your genuine self. Many people viewed as successful buy houses, trinkets, and toys, travel, eat more food than they need, get married or divorced, have a baby, or buy a puppy, all in the name of filling the void and finding that missing piece. Take note of these signs and ask if this is the case for you. People expressing their genuine selves also own real estate, have babies, buy puppies, and love toys. The difference is, these are not awards for achievements. They are things that come with ease to those who know who they are.

I speak from experience. I have had all the trappings of success and until recently, did not feel happy or at peace with these things. I have had investment properties, wonderful men in my life, and a fantastic family, enjoyed tropical vacations and romance, owned businesses, and received awards. I have had plenty of free time since I was in my mid-forties, yet none of this was enough to make me feel accomplished or good about who I was. It seemed that I needed to do more, that I was not enough. I felt there was more work to do, since I didn't know my purpose and I didn't feel my contribution to life was big enough. I was never at a place where I could look in the mirror and say that I was good enough, deserving of these honors. I accepted them humbly and gratefully, but never understood why I was selected.

The search to fill the void, the longing to finally take a day off and feel good about it, kept pushing me to explore who I really was. Everything was about being better at what I did and about being a better person. There seemed to be no point where I could relax and enjoy the day, knowing that I was enough. I had an overriding sense that something was missing, that something was preventing me from feeling that my successes were deserved. An old saying goes, "Fake it till you make it." I had made it but felt like I was faking it. I was embarrassed by all the attention and admiration from my peers and my clients. I had an overwhelming feeling that someday they would discover that I was not who they thought I was and that my world would crumble.

My self-esteem was as low as it could get for most of my adult life. The toys, the real estate, the travel, and the accolades did not ease my fear or release my anxiety. I attributed my struggle to feel confident to my history. My story tends to make people gasp in awe that I survived. But this response did not fill the void. I wanted to be loved and respected for being a kind, generous, intelligent woman, not a model of the tough survivor who accepts whatever happens to her.

That model, strong and going with the flow, brought me headaches, heartaches, and illness because it came with advice like: feel the fear and do it anyway; no pain, no gain; never let them see you sweat, and my favorite, fake it till you make it. I listened, I studied, I learned, and I applied what I had learned, and day after day, month after month, year after year I persisted in an attempt to improve who I was. Still, I repeated patterns that blindsided me after I thought I had conquered them. At times I felt that I would never be worthy of voicing my opinion or that I could trust my thoughts.

So often when I made a poor decision I found that I was repeating a pattern, even with the internal work I was committed to doing. I desired above all else to feel worthy and loved, and I assumed everyone who did not experience a tragic childhood knew more than I did. I would default to others' suggestions and discount my own ideas. It took me years to realize that many people also feel a void, believe they are not good enough, are unsure of themselves, and think others do not value what they contribute. Many of these people experienced happy childhoods, though just as many grew up in broken or blended families. Then there are those who spent their childhoods in environments saturated with addiction and anger. A dysfunctional childhood is not a prerequisite for feeling unworthy. This sense of unworthiness was not exclusive to me simply because by most people's standards my childhood was a horror story. I was convinced that there was something I was not seeing, a missing piece that I became more determined to find.

Finally, I had the revelation that my ego was holding on to self-defeating patterns, convincing me that I was not worthy, valuable, or wanted, and I recorded this experience. When I understood that my ego was preventing me from letting go of the past and embracing the truth of who I was, the void filled with love, joy, and positive energy.

I began to look at the world outside of my limited experience, and my journey to understand the human ego and the genuine self began. We are equally able to store pain, fear, and confusion and to feel love, joy, fulfillment, and confidence. So why are millions buying books, watching movies, attending seminars, and webinars, and forming support groups in search of that missing piece? What will fill the void sitting at the core of so many people?

With this revelation, I began to see people as individuals, doing the best they could with what they knew. I no longer relied on others to endorse my opinions. I valued what each person brought to the table and felt respect, knowing that we are all equals, no matter what our education or history. I saw that we can learn from one another, that we are all students and teachers, exchanging ideas and experiences. Understanding that there are no wrong answers, only the right one for myself and for others, released my anxieties and put an end to the judgments about myself. We cling to judgments because they give us a sense of power over others. In fact, they rob us of the peace of mind we desire. As long as we act as judge and jury over others, we will feel the need to know more and to be better than others to be worthy of love and respect. This is because those judgments we place on others we also place on ourselves, only without compassion.

The common cold provides an illustration. Imagine that you arrive at work in the morning and a gal in the office is feeling miserable because she has come down with a cold. Everyone tells her that she should have stayed home, that she needs to take care of herself.

When you wake up with a cold, you don't curl up in bed, thinking how you need to care for yourself. Instead you do everything possible to get into work, including taking drugs to control your symptoms. You tell yourself to toughen up and stop being a sissy; after all, it's only a cold. You worry about what others will think if you don't come to work. You need to be convinced that you will not be able to work under any circumstances before you will call in sick.

While you judge someone who takes time off for illness to be a weak person or someone taking advantage of others, you hold yourself to an even higher standard of judgment. You may feel guilt and shame for merely thinking you deserve to take time off.

Your ego holds a huge database of information for you to draw on to support your guilty feelings for thinking you should stay home and rest. The data provided by your ego will convince you not to take care of yourself, but to do as the propaganda that you have stored in your ego says: get up, get dressed, and stop feeling sorry for yourself just because you have a cold!

The reality is that you need to feel cared for, valued, worthy, and respected. You wouldn't take time off if you didn't need it. The voice making this argument is your genuine self, trying to be heard over the noisy voice of your ego. Why is it that once you drag yourself into work, feeling your worst, you can return home without guilt once your boss or colleagues give you the thumbs up? Wouldn't it be easier to listen to your genuine self and call in sick without the guilt? Rationally yes, but your ego lays the guilt on thick, and when you're not feeling strong and your guard is down, you don't want to fight, so you get out of bed, take enough drugs to fake it, and hope for the best.

This is the challenge of getting in step with the ego and letting your genuine self take the lead. The ego has many files in the data bank that remain hidden until an event such as a cold. Add to this that you have allowed the ego to send you to work every time you've had a cold, upset tummy, or headache in the past. This tells the ego to push harder and bombard you. The ego's job is to get you the information that corresponds with the event that you've stored, and the ego doesn't take its responsibilities lightly.

I decided that going forward I would replace my judgments of other people's habits with compassion and respect. What I think and believe is right for me, and what others think and believe is right for them. You can choose to change what you think and believe. If you have a cold, you can go back to bed, call in sick, and take care of yourself. And you can order those thoughts telling you that you are bad, wrong, or taking advantage of others to cease and desist!

For me, what matters most is that I can look myself in the mirror and feel I gave my best—that I was honest about what I thought and felt and respectful of those with whom I shared my day. In the end, it is myself to whom I must answer if I want to sleep without regret, or shame. I sleep well because I know I give my best each day. On those days when I am influenced by the old programming remaining in my ego data bank and I do something I am not proud of, I take note and promise to correct that defect in the programming. Then I sleep like a baby! The question you must ask every night is, did I honor my genuine self today by respecting my thoughts and by valuing my contributions? If not, ask why and find the answer to that question.

We probably wouldn't worry about what people think
of us if we could know how seldom they do.
—Olin Miller

I believe that what others think of me is none of my business. I don't have time to convince those who don't like me that they should, so I move on and let it go. People have the right to think and feel as they do. It's that simple. I know who I am and I know that I give my best to everyone and to all that I do. I also know that I can't change how other people think or feel, since they are operating from their own programming. This bit of clarity gives me the freedom to stop feeling I need to justify or defend myself. It also gives me strength. I keep in touch with my inner desire to be honest and fair, and check in with myself to be confident that I'm acting in accordance with this desire. I accept that not everyone will like me or agree with me, but that's okay, since I also don't like or agree with everyone I meet. The key is that I respect the right of others to be who they are, and understand that they are functioning from the programming they have learned during a lifetime of experiences.

You can also feel great about who you are. The key is to become aware of the effect of sitting in judgment of others. When you judge someone else, you are the only person shorted. It is fine to have an opinion very different from another person's, even when that opinion comes with passion. The key is to accept that these opinions are right for the parties holding them. Rigid judgment, the struggle for power, and the desire to be right cause frustration and negative energy and make you feel you must defend your opinion.

There are many people whom I don't respect or like, and I make it a point to spend as little time with them as possible. I don't get into debates with these people unless there is a benefit or need beyond my desire to be right. I accept that these people have as much right as I do to feel and act as they desire. Yes, dealing with these people is a trial; however, it isn't worth lowering my standards to fight with them. The impact of such battles on my genuine self would be far too costly. Fighting would conflict with my desire to be kind and compassionate. This stand is a bummer for my ego, which wants to win now and then to show others who's the toughest. When my ego pushes this desire, I remember the saying "If you wrestle with pigs, all you get is dirty," and I move on.

I realized some time ago that when we judge others we're actually holding ourselves up to judgment. You may walk down the street, see an obese person coming toward you, and think, *How can anyone let himself go like that?* You are expressing a judgment about body shape and size. If you are overweight or if you gain weight, you will be critical of yourself as well.

Many eating disorders result from people punishing themselves for gaining weight or not being their ideal weight. The truth may be that a person's weight increased due to a hormonal change, a crisis, stress, a change in eating habits, or aging. If you judge those who have weight issues to be uncaring, sloppy, disgusting, and inexcusably fat, you will impose these judgments on yourself. If you ever have a weight problem this will cause you to feel shame instead of confidence that you will get your weight back in line with your body. It is true in all cases that the judgments we hold for others we hold for ourselves, so be careful of your thoughts.

Your genuine self does not judge you or anyone else. It's your ego self that loves to play judge and jury. Become aware of this and add it to the list of actions and thoughts you will no longer allow yourself. Each time you have a judgmental thought about yourself or someone else, simply stop the thought. If you need to say "stop" out loud, do so. The thought will vanish, and over time these judgmental thoughts will diminish. This is a great tool for reprogramming your ego.

If you judge people, you have no time to love them.

—Mother Teresa

EXERCISE FOUR

1. List the judgments you have for others in the areas of career, relationships, health, mind (attitude), and body.

2. List the expectations you have for yourself in these areas.

3. Compare this list with the list of your characteristics and goals for who you want to be. Identify those that are not congruent with your genuine-self desires.

4. For the next twenty-one days, do one of the things on your genuine-self list of desires each day as often as you can. For example, if one of your desired characteristics is to be kind, for the next twenty-one days, do at least one new kind thing each day. Do this for all the action items on the list and watch how quickly the programming of your ego changes and the actions become automatic. Your new actions are what your ego will bring to your awareness in response.

For any judgment that you have discovered, take the same approach, with one difference. Instead of taking an action step for twenty-one days, find twenty-one reasons your judgment is not accurate. For example, you may judge that you don't need a man, since they are all self-centered and egotistical, with no respect for women. List twenty-one examples of the opposite. You may start by acknowledging that you need a man to open a pickle jar or to help you change a tire. It is important to list only the items that you believe to be true. Listing what you think are politically correct reasons will only feed your ego incorrect data. You may find this to be one of the most difficult assignments, because when we have faith that our beliefs are true, it is not easy to accept alternate possibilities. In any case, it is more than worth the time to do this exercise.

5. Repeat this process with all the items on your judgments list. It will get easier as you complete the list.

In summary, your ego will provide you with negative thoughts that make you feel defeated, inferior, and small. Your ego will tell you that you can't make it or get it right and that you must stay in your place and respect your limitations.

Your genuine self will support you in achieving whatever your heart desires. You will feel great about who you are and the things you do. You will have energy, smile more, and feel relaxed and confident. Remember this simple rule: if it feels good, do it more; if it hurts, stop doing it. Trust you genuine self, and the wisdom longing to be released will flow into every vein of your being. You will soon enjoy freedom of choice and the confidence to be your genuine self, taking the lead in life's dance.

Chapter 9

THE HYPNOTIC FACTORS

*Whether you think you can or think
you can't—you are right.*

—Henry Ford

*I*nternal and external influences are continually adding unwanted files to your ego's data bank. Many of these messages are subliminal and hypnotic, silently planting criticism that we too frequently turn into behaviors and beliefs. These emotionally charged thoughts enter our awareness without asking us to give them consideration. These messages slip quietly past our conscious mind and our cognitive awareness and into our subconscious mind. These messages are planted so deeply in our ego data bank that we do not give them thought before accepting them as attributes of our personal awareness. We don't evaluate whether these hypnotic suggestions are good for us.

Often we're not aware that we are doing things that could be harmful. How often do we robotically pick up the phone and order fast food when we're late getting dinner on the table or buy wrinkle cream because the gal on TV looked twenty-five years younger than her age? We habitually do these things without investigating the ingredients we are putting into our bodies or on our skin. We assume that someone or some system is in place to protect us.

This topic is controversial. Some say the food and drug protection agencies are self-serving and lax in their regulations. Others claim there is evidence to prove many products that we ingest and put on our skin are unsafe. Then there are those who challenge the labeling laws and note how misleading they can be. A mass of evidence has been marshaled on both sides of these arguments.

It is our responsibility to care enough about ourselves and our children to be confident in the choices we make. We should know the reasons we choose food, cleaning products, personal care products, and drugs. We should not respond robotically to commercials and buy into propaganda. We must be more confident in ourselves, trusting that we are more than capable of making good judgments about our well-being and do not need to be fixed, improved, or changed. We are just fine the way we are. We have control over what is stored in our ego mind. The problem is that we are often not aware of what is stored in the ego or how it is getting there.

Faced with so much propaganda designed to bypass our subconscious and conscious awareness, it is dangerous to ignore the impact this could have on our well-being and our desire to live authentic lives.

Let's agree that we will no longer be hypnotized by these subliminal messages. Let's stop automatically assuming that what our ego tells us to think is the truth. From this moment forward, let's agree to challenge our negative thoughts and emotions. Let's put our trust in our positive, kind thoughts and feelings and do our own thinking when it comes to how we feel about who we are. Let's also pay attention to our body. It knows what is good for us and alerts us when something is not so good.

People spend billions of dollars because they think they need to be improved, fixed, or made different. This is clear evidence of how deeply we are affected by subliminal messages! As Ernest Holmes said, "Practically the whole human race is hypnotized because it thinks what somebody else told it to think." That someone else includes television, magazines, the Internet, social media sites, and more, all available to us as apps on our cell phones. Each of these mediums brings us information on topics such as health and wellness, self-help, personal development, spirituality, money, religion, government, history, weight loss, anti-aging products, nutritional supplements, sex, addiction, natural and organic food, vacations, human rights, relationships, and finding our purpose, our passion, or our soul mate. There are many sites where you can shop, gamble, and socialize without leaving your chair.

Protected by our pass codes and user names, we are anonymous and reduced to statistics used to gather information for the market analysts to determine what we will buy next. The sheer volume of products we buy to improve ourselves is staggering. Are we really in such need of change that we must flock like sheep to buy every new product that brings us hope of achieving perfection?

What does this have to do with the ego? The ego is never asleep or separate from you, and is taking in and storing data 24-7, 365 days a year. While you are mindlessly watching a TV program to relax, eating junk food, and responding emotionally to what is on the screen, you are receiving new data in your ego database. When you react to something with an emotional charge, your ego stores that information. How often do we comment as we leave the office that we are going to veg out in front of the TV tonight? We head home excited about having some me time. We stop on the way to pick up our favorite snack foods. Viewed rationally, how is this activity good for you? When you eat junk food in the evening while mindlessly watching TV, you are developing a habit that is for many very difficult to break. Yet, even though we all agree that this is not a habit that is good for our well-being, we not only get excited, we share this excitement with our friends, inviting them to join us! We all agree that we work hard, and we feel that if we forgo life's pleasures, we will be condemned to restrictive, repressed lives. We believe that this no way to live.

We conclude that deprivation leads to a life of scarcity and ugliness. Then, feeling justified, we turn our attention to our favorite TV show and take that first bite of comfort food. Assured that we are doing this to spoil ourselves a little, to indulge in the good things that life has to offer, we purr like kittens. Just how did we buy into abusing ourselves in the guise of loving and honoring ourselves and satisfying our needs? Have we so lost sight of what makes us feel good that we think we need junk food and external stimulation from TV, movies, and the Internet to feel special, to affirm that we care about ourselves? Although we know that these habits do nothing good for us, we stand our ground, claiming that we are entitled to an evening in front of the TV with our favorite comfort foods and our friends.

Where, how, and when did we make this decision? What about this behavior is healthy for us physically, emotionally, spiritually, or mentally? Pay attention to how you answer these questions, because if you are convinced these habits are in any way good for you, you have been brainwashed. You are now the media and advertising world's puppet! If you are okay with having the propaganda makers take over your mind, you do not need to read any further. If this scares the hell out of you, read on!

Corporations and the media rely on our emotional triggers to get us to buy their products, listen to their stories, and watch their programs. Our rational mind usually tells us something very different than to satisfy our emotional desire and grab that bag of chips, buy that shiny new food processer, or purchase a hundred pairs of socks, fifty free (shipping and handling extra). Many of us have drawers full of socks, and yet we can't say no! We know this is advertising designed to pull us in, but our emotions, combined with the ego's awareness, sell us on the idea. We feel good when we buy new things; this is the hook that instantly overrides our logic.

Along with the placement of the latest order, the ego has stored another example of when you ordered new stuff from the TV or online. The ego records how this made you feel, so if you begin to think that the item on the TV commercial is not so great, your ego will retrieve the data on buying socks and remind you of this experience and the emotions that came with it. The ego is a gullible, naïve softie, like a child without guidance, and does not have the capability to question whether information is harmful or good for you. Your ego doesn't have an opinion on what data you choose to store. It simply stores the information you feed it, without judgment or question. You cannot turn off your ego. It is with you 24-7 and is storing data the entire time. While you sleep, while you are awake, and yes, while you are watching TV and eating comfort foods. Would you allow a two-year-old to sit up all night eating junk food? Why do you allow yourself to do it? The difference is that your ego doesn't get sick. Your body does!

Another problem to consider is information overload. Richard Wurman, author of *Information Anxiety* (Doubleday, 1989), claims that a weekday edition of the *New York Times* contains more information than the average person in seventeenth-century

England was likely to come across in a lifetime. It is estimated that more information has been produced in the last thirty years than in the previous five thousand.

Given all the information available in the electronic age, people feel overwhelmed and worn down with so much coming at them all the time. When our energy is low, we don't think as clearly, we are not as strong, and we often find ourselves making choices to get challenges off of our plates so we can move on to the next demand. We must respect ourselves enough to walk away from anything that no longer serves us or makes us happy, even if our peers, family, and friends do not agree.

I have chosen the topic of health and wellness to demonstrate the hypnotic effect of messages filled with propaganda to which we are exposed to twenty-four hours a day, seven days a week, and fifty-two weeks a year.

The focus on changing our body, our looks, our size, our energy level, and our health drives one of the biggest industries in North America. We all want to feel that we are politically correct and current when choosing fashion, accessories, food, gyms, exercise programs, diets, careers, partners, and friends. We want to be healthy, live longer, and stay young. This means we need wrinkle cream, hormone replacement programs, nutritional supplements, face-lifts, Botox treatments, bigger breasts, smaller thighs, fuller lips, and whiter teeth, and gray hair is unacceptable for women until they are at least ninety-five. We live in fear of suffering with arthritis, asthma, coronary disease, and cancer. We also face the West Nile virus and the superbugs. When are we safe? When will we be okay as we are? When can we stop being afraid of what is next?

Are you aware that the number-three killer of men, women, and children in North America today is prescription drugs? Still, we line up faithfully to fill our prescriptions, hoping we are immune from the side effects listed for the miracle drugs that will fix our ailments. Then we search for the best insurance plan we can get, in case we find ourselves incapacitated and unable to work due to the many illnesses that can take us down. How often do we hear people respond to an ache or pain with the acknowledgment that this is how life is after we turn forty?

Whatever happened to relying on one's immune system instead of popping pills and smearing on creams? We are living longer and epidemics have been fewer with modern medicine, which is a good thing; however, the pendulum has swung too far out of balance and we now rely on pharmaceuticals to solve the slightest malady instead of riding it out and strengthening our immune systems. We do not want to take a day off from work or mess up our schedules by being ill. That just causes more stress!

Have you heard about the superbugs that are resistant to antibiotics and could cause an epidemic that wipes out millions of people? This is the result of the overuse of antibiotics by humans on all commercially raised animals and fish. It concerns me when I hear news broadcasts that say scientists are close to marketing a pill for relieving the discomfort of grief or resolving shyness in children. What happened to being allowed to feel whatever you feel and learning how to deal with that? Why are we moving toward feeling numb, our bodies held together with plastic and metal parts, and popping pills as a solution to whatever ails us? Why are we allowing this? Is it because we are hypnotized, letting others influence us and dictate what is best for us instead of thinking for ourselves. What happened to questioning and deciding for ourselves, trusting our inner wisdom, going within, accessing and listening to our source, available at the core of each of us? We don't need to hide, numb out, or live in fear. We simply need to allow ourselves to be present. We must listen to the core awareness in our subconscious and conscious minds and no longer allow messages to be added to the ego database without our approval.

I am fifty-eight as I write this book; I came from a destructive childhood and have experienced countless disappointments and betrayals. At one time I was diagnosed with as many as 114 environmental allergies and 225 food allergies, and my doctors told me I was overweight because of a lack of discipline. I had my appendix removed, suffered a few broken bones, was a chronic asthmatic, was diagnosed with panic disorder, and had heart arrhythmia and a brain tumor. All this by the time I was forty! With these ailments, one would expect that I have a medicine cabinet lined with prescription bottles and creams and that my medical expenses are through the roof.

How is it that today I am healthier and stronger than ever? I do not have a benefit or medical insurance plan. I have not had the flu, a cold, or other ailment for about fifteen years. I have experienced the odd stiff neck, sore throat, or sniffle, and when these occur I look at what I have been eating, review my stress factors, and ask myself how I am feeling emotionally. Since 1995, I have not used an inhaler, a breathing machine, or an antibiotic. I use nutritional supplements and I eat a whole-foods diet. I do not smoke, I rarely drink, and I do not allow the use of chemical products in my home or office or on my body. I live on property with well water and never use herbicides or pesticides. I chose hardwood floors and no carpets, sleep on a mattress without fire retardants, and have few window treatments, or furniture that contains pressed wood in my home.

I am considered odd and a bit fanatical when it comes to what I will eat and am teased over my desire to live free of toxins in my home. I use true essential oils, but not scented candles. I say no to processed foods and yes to good quality meats and veggies. I do not drink coffee, juice, or pop, and I rarely eat sugar, sweets, or junk foods. It is easy to track what adds weight when I am respecting what I know to be true for my body's needs. For example, I can eat cheddar cheese, but I will have brain fog that day. So I limit how often I have cheddar cheese. I can have cottage cheese or goat cheese without adverse effects. I will wake up congested when I eat things that contain flour; it makes no difference if it is ancient grains, wheat, oats, barley, or gluten-free. Grains, finely ground into a flour state, are one of those foods that I keep to a minimum in my diet because when I eat them I feel sleepy, am easily distracted, and of course gain weight.

I find it interesting that when I respect the fact that certain foods don't do well in my body, I have no desire for them. Once I choose to have cheddar cheese or a slice of bread, my body will crave this food for two to three days before the yearning subsides. I rarely give in, because it is not worth the side effects of brain fog, loss of energy, and weight gain. I also find it annoying to keep saying no to a craving for those few days. I know the process I need to implement to get back on track. With this I am free to eat whatever I want; I do not often want foods that are not good for me.

Even with this knowledge, I was hypnotized by propaganda for five years and gained fifty pounds. I tried many programs to address the weight gain. Each one brought the same results. I would lose some weight, but it would always return and I would weigh more than I did before trying the program. I was buying into propaganda about diet plans, weight management, and healthy eating, going from one to the other, desperately wanting my flexible, strong body back. I understood how easy it is to get sidetracked and the difficulty of starting over, but more than anything, I learned that I was listening to propaganda about body image, healthy eating habits, and foods defined as healthy choices by marketing gurus. I was not listening to my body, which holds wisdom on what is good for me and what is not. It is my body that gets headaches, sore joints, muscle pains, and brain fog. The causes of my body responses are not the same as the causes in others, so a one-size-fits-all solution is a crap shoot. You might get lucky, but many of us with weight management challenges will attest that if a plan isn't right for you, the weight comes back, plus a little more.

After returning to what I know, listening to my body, and respecting its likes and dislikes, I lost twenty of those fifty pounds in only six weeks. The key is listening to the body and loving it enough to protect it from things that cause stress and bring harm, including many of the comfort foods and "healthy" foods that we let industry propaganda sell us. I feel so good and so strong that my ego does not even hear the messages, subliminally or otherwise. I enjoy my favorite comfy foods now and then, but only by choice. Strangely, they rarely have the same effect on my body, but they no longer comfort me either, so there are no feelings of loss or deprivation associated with saying no. I feel good, strong, and flexible. If I get a pain or feel out of sorts, I examine what I ate and my day's actions and correct my course. It really is that easy.

The toughest part is learning to hear what your body is telling you. To do this, you need to be clear whether you are listening to your ego or your genuine self. I do not watch a lot of TV or spend time on the Internet. I am selective about what I expose myself to physically, mentally, spiritually, and emotionally, since I know how easily I am influenced by propaganda. I am an emotional and sensitive person, so it is easy to imagine how good the food in a commercial will taste. For a time, I needed to treat commercials as if I were an addict hooked on watching them. I had to avoid viewing them and not allow them into my energy field. I can handle a few, but not many. To do this, I needed to stop watching TV, and to this day I limit my viewing to no more than two hours each day. I rarely watch that much. I feel that I owe myself this, since I am more important than a TV show. I watch programs and movies that come in boxed sets. These are not filled with commercials.

Being aware that I am influenced by these hypnotic factors has allowed me to take charge of how I manage this unsolicited data. My ego self will store what I listen to when I am emotionally relating to it. When a commercial for food comes on, I am now able to focus my thoughts and emotions on what I know will be my body reaction. Foods presented in the commercials are no longer calling my name, begging me to try them. The ability to resist these ploys is an amazing and empowering thing. In return, I have a strong, healthy body and a wonderful immune system. Recently, a naturopathic doctor told me that people would pay a thousand dollars for a drop of my blood because my immune system is in the ninety-seventh percentile. It felt good to be complimented for the efforts I have made to take charge of my health. Stress, internal dialogue, and external messages coming from all directions have an impact on our wellness. We are not immune to these external influences; however, we are hypnotized by them only when we do not listen to and respect our genuine self.

EXERCISE FIVE

1. Visualize yourself as vital, the perfect size for your body type, glowing, strong, and doing the things that you love to do. Visualize this ideal self every day.

2. Create a storyboard with all the fashions, colors, activities, foods, and other things that you love. Build this storyboard around your vision of your healthy self.

3. Put the storyboard in a place where you can see it, possibly your sanctuary or private space, and study it. Feel the pleasure it brings; then close your eyes and see it come to life in your mind. Invite your imagination to taste the foods, touch your favorite outfit, and feel how well it fits your body. Do the activities as you are in this space, and wrap your arms around yourself as you feel the joy and wonder of being there.

4. Make the commitment to do this exercise as often as you can in a week. The more often you do this, the sooner you will feel the changes happening deep within as your old ego programming is replaced with the new data about who you are.

When we ignore our own desires and listen to the propaganda bombarding us from all directions, many of us feel trapped without hope. We must ask questions and explore alternatives instead of believing what we read or what we are told by experts, including doctors, reporters, celebrities, and writers touting products. The goal of advertisers, who have billions of dollars in their budgets, is to sell us on why we need these products. These brilliant promotions are designed to appeal to our fear of getting older or dying from some horrible disease and to our vanity, which tells us we can't look a day over twenty-two and be considered beautiful or sexy. If we listen to commercials, read popular publications, or hear people talking in restaurants or at social gatherings, we will observe how many of us are placing judgment on those we know.

Conversations are often critical and unforgiving. With all these sources continually providing data, our ego receives more than enough negative information to store in our awareness. Once we realize how much is being stored, change can sound impossible. The key point to remember is that when you decide to no longer accept these messages as true for you, your ego will update your programming and then test if you really want it updated. Be prepared. The ego will use what was stored through all the propaganda to challenge you with a vengeance as you begin reprogramming. Knowing this will shield you as you undertake the process. Don't let this challenge from your ego discourage or sidetrack you. Be ready so that when you allow yourself to feel how wonderful and beautiful you are and your ego tries to dismiss these thoughts, you will know that the ego is testing your new awareness of who you are. You must have a plan to respond when these old perceptions are brought to the forefront.

Following the steps I am about to share will enable you to reprogram your ego with fewer challenges. This process is the cumulative result of reading three books, *The Biology of Belief* by Bruce H. Lipton, *Change Your Brain, Change Your Body* by Daniel G. Amen, and *Virus of the Mind* by Richard Brodie. Each clarified my understanding of how our brain and beliefs work to create outcomes in our lives. In the coaching training that I have done, I learned that the focus of any change is to remove blocks and replace them with data supporting what we want to achieve. I also learned that planning before you take action results in greater and more permanent success. I would like to share what I found valuable in each of these books. They helped bring substantial change in my life, giving me the freedom and the courage to be my genuine self. I strongly recommend you read these books, since I am sharing only what worked for me. We are all uniquely individual, and there may be more in these books for you to discover.

In *The Biology of Belief*, Lipton tells of his experiences in challenging the traditional teachings of medical school and shares his discoveries about the impact belief can have on our environment, including the body. He notes how we can change a belief and then see a change in our body and the world around us.

In *Change Your Brain, Change Your Body*, Amen recounts how researchers have discovered through brain imaging that our emotional and physical states, like our mental state, can have an impact on a brain scan. When we correct an emotional, physical, or mental issue, the brain changes and heals. Amen has evidence that negative thoughts affect the brain and that when these are changed, the brain corrects itself. His program includes many exercises that identify brain types and isolate issues affecting the brain, and he offers a wonderful process for clearing out negative thoughts.

In *Virus of the Mind*, Brodie identifies the mental viruses that he calls memes, which are the beliefs we inherit from our parents, our past lives, and influences such as the media and advertising. He refers to these as viruses because they spread from one generation to the next.

Combining the information from these three amazing men, I discovered that it is possible to move forward with confidence, fully aware that our thoughts create our experiences. How often have we heard the expression "Thoughts are things" and wondered what that means for us? We know that we are not genies who blink and make things appear. These three books show how we are affected by thoughts and how these thoughts come to be things in our life experiences. Thoughts are founded on information we have obtained throughout our lives. We store these thoughts in our ego mind. We share one planet, but we each have our own unique environment within us and around us. We are affected by the world around us, and the desires within us are often overshadowed by the massive bombardment of data coming from the outer world, propaganda as I call it. We now know that we can change our brain and our body. We also can change our beliefs to change our environment; the mind viruses that we have inherited can be reprogrammed and silenced so that we can hear the voice of our genuine self. This self provides us with thoughts that support us as we express who we truly are.

Before I share exercise six, which will provide you with a wonderful process that I still use every time I need help sorting out my thoughts, I want to note that when I mention being the best you that you can be and living a life filled with what you desire, I am not talking about entitlement or being superior to anyone else. This process is not about winning a competition or outdoing someone. It is about freeing what is in your core being that is longing to be set free. It is about freeing that part within you that loves and appreciates you and cherishes the world you live in. You must look beyond the surface that your ego presents as your life. This is what is meant by awareness, your beliefs about who you are. You must challenge the strength of your beliefs and be brutally honest when recording what is going on in your thoughts and emotions, even when it seems foolish or embarrassing. You must search to find what is of real value to you, beyond the material desires you thought gave you an identity. This commitment to get to know yourself beyond what you know today will free you and create the results you seek.

Be proud to wear you.

—Dodinsky

This next exercise contains eight steps that will take you through a process of defining your thoughts. The goal is to see ego thought and genuine thought. I will use this process in two examples to provide guidance as you apply this exercise to your thoughts.

Use this process when you are spending time reminding yourself that you are fine the way you are but you are experiencing days when you feel that you have no value, aren't smart enough, good enough, or pretty enough, or deserving. If any of this thinking is occupying your mind, then you must question your statement that nothing needs to change, since your habits and your actions are not in agreement. When you have these critical thoughts, you might be feeling disappointed, out of sorts, lonely, lost, or tired of the same old grind. These are all clues that your self-awareness is focused on the negative. When this is the case, you are denying that things could be different, blocking yourself from feeling the truth that you look fabulous and are smart and deserving. You are missing out on feeling confident and sexy. When you see yourself as needing improvement and make this the rationale for why you feel discouraged, stuck, or any of the many negative feelings that come with self-criticism, you could soon find yourself planning for tummy tucks or tooth capping, a new nose or breast enhancements. Somehow all these options start to sound appealing. Using this process, you should explore why you feel these changes would improve you.

The process will help you examine why you believe that the solution to all your problems is attached to how you look, as an example. If you think that looks are the solution, by the way, notice how many supermodels and movie stars die prematurely from drug overdoses. These are physically perfect people, so why don't they have perfect lives, filled with peace, joy, and love? This alone should make people question why they have accepted the thought that improving how they look would improve their lives. Of course we all need to care about our personal hygiene and grooming. I am not suggesting that we let ourselves go, stop bathing or taking care of our bodies, or dress as if we don't care about how we look. I am saying that our noses, eyes, arms, legs, bellies, hair, and hairlines are all just fine.

If you have concluded that you need to improve who you are, it is because your ego has been storing the propaganda that bombards you each day, convincing you that you need to be fixed so that you buy products. When you know at your very core that you are beautiful, you will reprogram the data your ego holds and quickly and easily eliminate any negative information that finds its way into your database. You will no longer feel that your disappointment stems from how you look or dress; you will know that you have presented your best self, your genuine self, and let it go. All healthy people want to look and feel their best, and if a nose job has a real benefit, and isn't a response to the opinions of others, then you must do what is best for you. Reconstructive surgery after a car accident, for example, is necessary. People who are critical of another person's appearance are not in touch with their genuine selves and therefore should not be the measure for your personal awareness. If you live fully present, you will be aware of yourself and others in a very different way, and the opinions of others will not outweigh what you know is true about yourself. All this said, listen carefully to your self-dialogue as you answer the questions in this process. The goal is to recognize when you are listening to your genuine self versus your ego self.

EXERCISE SIX

The following questions will assist you in determining whether your desires and beliefs are coming from the data bank of your ego or from your genuine-self desire. These questions will bring clarity to issues you face and help you discover whether you are listening to your ego or your genuine self. You will no longer be affected by hypnotic factors and will make the choices that best serve you. Follow this eight-step process:

1. Statement: I _____

    _____

2. Is this statement true? Spiritually, mentally, physically, and emotionally the absolute truth with no exceptions or other possibilities? Yes or no?

3. If the answer is yes, that your statement is the absolute truth and you respond or act accepting that it is the truth, then you feel …

4. If the answer is no, that your statement is not the absolute truth and you respond or act accepting that it is not the truth, then you feel …

5. Which of these two choices made you feel empowered and pleased with having respected yourself? (Observe how great it feels to accept the truth about this situation. You chose which option to accept, the absolute truth or the excuses disguised as truths, and benefited by being empowered when honoring what is true.)

6. I accept that my statement blocked me from seeing the truth by …

7. What action(s) will I take when a thought blocks me from hearing my genuine self?

8. My genuine self and my ego self now know that the reality of this issue is that …

EXAMPLE ONE:

I'll use the example of thoughts that followed a job interview, applied to this process. Thought while driving home after the interview: *If I had worn the dress instead of the black suit, I would have made a better impression.*

1. Statement: I am sure that I would have made a better impression if I was wearing a dress at this interview instead of the black suit. I should have known better. What was I thinking?

2. Is my choosing the black suit over a dress absolutely a mistake? Is this beyond a doubt spiritually, mentally, physically, and emotionally the truth, with no exceptions or other possibilities? I could not make a great impression wearing the black suit and there was no chance of getting this job because I wore that suit to the interview?

   Response: No. Of course it is not definitively true. It isn't possible to know that this is what the interviewer thought, although I think I could have made a better impression by wearing a dress instead of my black suit. I might have felt more confident during the interview, but I don't know that for sure. Therefore this statement is not true at all. Further, I cannot say that wearing a dress instead of my black suit would have made any difference. I do not know that for sure. I was quite nervous before I got to the interview.

3. If I agree that it is the absolute truth that choosing the black suit over the dress is why I have no chance of getting this job, it makes me feel …

Response: Frustrated, because although it may be absolutely true that wearing the dress could have presented me in a better light, there is no way for me to make the right choice before going on an interview. It may be true that the reason I did not make a good impression was my choice of outfit, but how am I to know what the perfect outfit is from the interviewer's perspective? All I can do is present my best. I should not be expected to know the interviewer's taste in attire. I looked professional and well put together in the black suit. Portraying me as a loser because I didn't know what the interviewer would think is unreasonable. In any case, if this statement is true, maybe I should stop looking for work. Who would hire someone who doesn't even know what to wear to the interview? Now I am depressed.

4. If I agree that it is not the absolute truth that choosing the black suit over the dress made a bad impression, then I feel …

Response: If it is not true that wearing the black suit was a bad choice or made a difference, then I can feel good about how I presented myself. I chose that suit because it made me feel feminine and professional. My hair was fabulous, and I knew I would be a great fit for anyone looking for a person to work in a professional setting. I presented myself well and gave my best. I can feel great about myself! I was nervous, but that is expected when somebody wants a job as much as I did this one. I know I presented myself with the best intentions, and am proud that I did not let my nerves get the better of me.

5. Which of these observations do you accept as the truth in this situation?

   Response: That it is absolutely not true. I can't find any argument to support that this is a truth in this situation.

6. I accept that my statement blocked me from seeing the truth by …

   Raising the possibility that this dress could have made a difference. My thoughts were on the dress, not on my lack of confidence. By blaming my choice of outfit, I do not need to look at what I did right or could improve on. The focus on the outfit skews my perspective. I am feeling sad and disappointed and I don't even know if I will be offered the position, because my thoughts and emotions are caught up in being critical of the outfit I chose.

7. What action(s) will I take the next time a thought blocks me from listening to my genuine self?

   Response: I will stop the thought the instant I recognize it and remind myself of how great I looked and how thoughtfully I prepared for that interview. In other words, I will immediately find my favorite thoughts about myself to replace the negative, critical ones.

I will use this eight-step process to break the thoughts into small pieces so I can regain my perspective.

I will keep a journal of my positive attributes and focus on these each day.

8. I trust that my genuine self knows the truth about …

This issue because it feels good and empowering to see how silly I was to think that a dress could make or break an interview. My mind was churning out nonsense. I was well groomed and put care and pride into my selection of hairstyle, outfit, shoes, makeup, and accessories, and for my ego mind to tell me this was not good enough is not acceptable. It is laughable when I think about it. I made great choices in preparing for the interview. I will not let the negative thoughts presented by my ego's awareness rain on my parade. It is irritating to think that my own ego would be so critical, knowing how nervous I was about this interview.

Commentary on example one:

After completing the process using the example of the selection of an outfit for a job interview, can you see how the focus of the ego mind imposed doubt, loss of confidence, and an overall sense of loss and poor performance? Can you see how the person's belief that the dress would have made the difference changed as the questions in this process were answered? Can you see how her personal environment went from doubtful to confident and pleased with herself as she completed the process? Do you agree that this process neutralized her negative thoughts, replacing them with positive, supportive thoughts, and allowed genuine self-awareness to prevail over the ego awareness?

If I am not for myself, who will be?

—Pirke Avoth

EXAMPLE TWO

You are walking by a bakery and a tray of chocolate fudge brownies catches your eye. You are committed to making healthy food choices, but this is the thought that might enter your mind to rationalize having a brownie.

1. Statement: I want a brownie. I have not had a brownie for at least six months, so having one today will not hurt me.

2. Is this statement beyond a doubt absolutely true, spiritually, mentally, physically, and emotionally, with no exceptions or other possibilities?

    Response: No. You chose to avoid eating sweets for the past six months because you believed them to be made of ingredients high in sugar and possibly of additives that are not healthy choices. Since you last chose to have sweets six months ago, there has been no change in the fact that brownies are not a healthy food choice. The fact that your body has not had a brownie for a long time does not make the brownie less harmful. No, eating a brownie after six months is no different to your body than having one yesterday.

3. If I agree that this statement is the absolute truth, it makes me feel …

    Response: It makes me feel that I am not respecting my body and that I am making excuses to justify eating food that I know is not healthy. After I eat the brownie and feel that pleasure for a moment or two, I will feel sad, knowing that have let myself down. I will no longer feel the excitement of being in control and making healthy choices when it comes to sweets.

4. If I agree that this statement is not the absolute truth, it makes me feel …

Response: It makes me feel strong, confident, and great because I know I am in control of what I choose to put into my body. It feels good to be aware of the impact that the brownie will have on my body if I choose to eat it. I feel pleased with myself for respecting my body, knowing that there is never a great time to eat food that is not good for me, no matter how much I might want it.

5. Which of these observations do I accept as the truth in this situation?

Response: The truth is that the brownie is no healthier a food choice just because it has been six months since I had one. It feels great to be able to make this choice with confidence and to respect my body.

6. I accept that my statement blocked me from seeing the truth by …

Response: I was blocked by thoughts derived from the old data in my ego reminding me of the pleasure of eating sweets and giving me the idea that if six months has passed, it would be okay to have a brownie. These thoughts told me I could do this in good conscience, since this qualified as a healthy food choice because I did not eat brownies more often.

7. What action(s) will I take the next time such thoughts block me from listening to my genuine self?

Response: If I have this thought again, I will remind myself how great and empowering it felt to say no to that brownie, and remember that the feeling of being empowered and in control of my life lasted a lot longer than a few quick bites of a brownie.

I will not say yes to any cookies, donuts, cakes, pies, brownies, or other sweets on impulse. I will stop and run the thought through this process before deciding whether to eat these foods.

8. My genuine self and my ego self now agree that the reality of this issue for me is that I love feeling confident and empowered as I make healthy choices about the foods I put into my body.

Commentary on example two:

It is now easy to draw on the idea that the chocolate fudge brownie did not become a healthy food because you didn't eat one for six months, and this truth can now apply to the thought that any unhealthy food is okay in moderation. Your ego mind will present both options until you choose which you favor. Before long, you will not be attracted to the foods you do not want to put into your body.

The simple process demonstrated in exercise six will help you to change your perception on any question and take control in dealing with issues. The key is to listen to your thoughts. Recognizing when your genuine self is speaking can be difficult. Be patient with yourself as you practice. With this process you will move forward confidently and no longer allow your ego to present critical thoughts to you without resistance. Your commitment to replace these negative thoughts with positive, supportive thoughts about yourself will help you reprogram your ego.

In the beginning, your ego will take every opportunity to remind you of those old negative thoughts, but each time you are feeling picked on or stuck, use this process to bring the correct perspective to the issue and your ego will soon be programmed and flowing in unison with your genuine self. Using this process, you will encounter times when you find more negative thoughts attached to the thought you noted in your opening statement. When this happens, take note of these thoughts and apply the process to them one at a time. You will soon feel shielded from propaganda, no longer attracted to its charm and seductive messages. You will feel the energy that comes from feeling you're free and empowered to make your own choices.

*I am not afraid of storms for I am
learning how to sail my ship.*

—Louisa May Alcott

Chapter 10

EXTERNAL INFLUENCES

Put your future in good hands - your own.

—Author Unknown

*Y*ou now have a process to assist you in neutralizing negative thought patterns and in replacing those judgments with thoughts true for you. You also know how to recognize when you are responding to your ego's messages instead of thoughts from your genuine self-awareness. You are well on your way to personal freedom!

As we explore a few of the external influences commonly stored in our ego's data bank, apply the processes and exercises introduced thus far. You are now also aware of the hypnotic factors and the impact that information overload has on the data stored in your ego mind.

Exploring external and internal influences will provide insight into the streams of negative information flowing in our culture and around the world. To complete your personal work, it is important to narrow down and become aware of the negative thoughts that are influencing you.

Awareness is the key to unlocking the door to your genuine self and living a life of personal freedom. Information expands our awareness, so let's begin by exploring a few external influences to which we are exposed every day in many subtle ways. External influences are those messages that come from the environment outside our own mind, body, and soul.

Pat yourself on the back and celebrate that you have the courage to walk away from what no longer serves you and makes you happy. You owe yourself this opportunity to grow and to be happy, out of respect for who you are.

EXERCISE SEVEN

As you look at the following ten external influences, take note of any thoughts that resonate with you. Take note, too, of your emotions and any physical reactions such as chills or warm feelings. Determine whether this information makes you feel stronger, happier, positive, excited, sad, weak, or some other way.

If you feel more energized, alert, and alive, keep those moments of joy and peace coming. Add the actions that produce these great new feelings to your daily to-do list and increase the frequency whenever possible.

To explore external influences, I have chosen common categories that involve billions of dollars and generate much propaganda. The messages delivered by these external influences are stored in the files that our ego holds for us on how we look, feel, and present ourselves. There are many topics that I have not touched on, but the approach I use here is transferable to any topic you choose. The goal is to get you thinking about things that you have accepted as true. If you believe by default that something is true, then you believe it is true for you, making this a part of your awareness. Your perception is your reality.

EXTERNAL INFLUENCE ONE: HEALTH

I have chosen health as the first topic because this category is at the top in attracting money from people seeking solutions. Without health, nothing else matters. Living with disease or the fear of disease places many limits on those suffering from compromised health and those sharing their lives.

My health has been compromised more than once, and each time it happened, my quality of life deteriorated. It became critical for me to look beyond the surface, beyond the obvious, to improve and strengthen my health. I succeeded and today I have an amazing immune system, strong bones, healthy eyes, no hearing problems, no aching joints or headaches, great energy, and a strong heart. I am in tune with my body.

This was one of my biggest journeys, and it took me through layers of discovery. In my early thirties, my health was deteriorating quickly. I had gained fifty pounds in only ninety days. My asthma reached a chronic level, requiring me to carry two inhalers and spend time on a breathing machine at least once every thirty days. My body was giving up, and I was in and out of hospitals, on cardio machines, put on numerous drugs for anxiety, and had difficulty staying awake for more than four hours at a time. I was weak, exhausted, and mentally tired. Taking a deep breath was difficult. My ability to think and to concentrate was severely diminished. I was a single parent of three with no family or financial support. I was scared, alone, and vulnerable.

When I was thirty-five, I developed a severe pain in my right temple, lost my hearing, and experienced blurred vision in my right eye. I delayed going to the doctor because I could not afford to take time off from work. I was struggling to manage and did not have the energy or the money to add more prescribed drugs to my budget. Finally, in the fall of 1989, when the pain was so bad I could no longer function, I sought medical attention, and on November 5, 1989, I was told that I had a brain tumor. I still remember the pale green walls of that hospital room and the muffled voices speaking. I was not able to clearly comprehend their words in the shock of that moment. When I snapped back into the room, I understood that they wanted to rush me into surgery, which I could not agree to do. I had kids who had nowhere to go and no one to care for them. But after much arguing and after listening to the doctors explain that I was risking my life, I signed the papers accepting the risks and ensuring them that I would not hold them or the hospital liable should something happen to me. Then I headed home.

I cried for the next two or three days, and then I got to work. I needed to make enough money to pay for my home and my kids until I recovered, which the doctors told me would take about ten months. I focused on working, making money, cooking meals and freezing them, and making arrangements to care for the kids. By the end of March 1990, close to five months later, I achieved my goals and had enough money to keep me going for the ten months I needed to recover. Throughout those five months, I was frequently in the hospital. I agreed to have the doctors monitor the tumor, and to everyone's surprise, it did not grow. In December 1989, one month after my diagnosis, my mother agreed to come from Vancouver and help me prepare and freeze food. This visit was extremely painful for me because our relationship was very difficult. We cooked and packed up food for the freezer, using the ingredients that I bought with the little money I had, and when we were done, she told me she was taking the food to my sister, who needed her help. She told me that I would be fine and that I should have not have divorced my husband if I didn't want to be on my own; my sister had never married but somehow had not chosen to be on her own. I won't bore you with how angry I was; however, my mother did not hear from me for nearly five years after that event. Once again, I needed her and she wasn't there for me.

After I left Vancouver at twenty-one, my mother and I rarely spoke or spent time together. On the rare occasion that we did speak, I had to be strong emotionally. A year before the tumor, along with developing asthma, gaining weight, and struggling to get my life back on track financially after my divorce, I started having flashbacks, which turned out to be memories from my childhood. I had not remembered my childhood until I began experiencing these flashbacks. Until then, I thought I was like anyone else with an alcoholic father and a mother, who was trying desperately to cope with five kids and no money.

When this first flashback occurred, I was working as a Realtor and was showing a couple an older home, which had a dirt cellar. I lifted the trapdoor in the kitchen floor, exposing stairs that descended into the cellar, and as I reached to brace the cover with a stick, I had a flash of myself being locked in a cellar. I could feel the bugs and mice crawling and squeaking, I saw the perfect yellow dress I was wearing, and I knew I would be in trouble if I got it dirty. I heard my mother telling me to turn off the lights and do my thinking in the dark. This was the beginning of many flashes of memories and the increasing panic attacks and health issues that followed.

I did not know these were memories at first and was convinced I was mentally ill in addition to my failing physical health. I sought counseling for a short period until the person I was seeing pointed out that I could recover only if I were willing to recall and relive all these traumatic events.

Listening to my inner voice for the first time, I declared that I could see no benefit from reliving these horrifying events or dredging up old fears. What I really needed was to know how to appropriately respond so that the panic attacks and fears would no longer have such control or such a debilitating affect. The therapist did not agree, so I paid her for her time and that was that. She had also told me that given the severity of the sexual abuse I had experienced, I could never have a healthy sexual relationship. I called this the most absurd statement I had ever heard. I was a child who had no control over what was done to me by the adults in my life. I refused to accept that I should feel ashamed, guilty, or defective for the rest of my life for something I could not stop. I was interested in finding out what healthy sexual habits and behaviors were. Feeling at a loss and not knowing where to turn, I went to the public library and to bookstores.

I did not feel I could share what was happening with the people around me. I had quickly discovered that if I did, they often treated me as if I were contagious and they would somehow catch abuse. This left me feeling isolated as well as scared, confused, insignificant, and unwanted.

As this series of events occurred, I began observing that each time I saw a doctor or a therapist or visited a clinic or hospital, I would get more negative news, a list of things to worry about or prepare for, and often more prescribed drugs. Never was I asked about my emotional health. No one asked if I was having difficulties in my life. Everyone focused on the physical effects of the anxiety, my regular bouts of heart arrhythmia, and my breathing issues. Today, having done a lot of research on trauma and recovery, I realize I had all the symptoms of post-traumatic stress, and yet these experts, whose care I was under, had not considered that possibility.

To make matters worse, when I started asking about this possibility, I soon found myself tagged in the medical system computers as a hypochondriac and as someone who shopped for doctors, looking for one who would prescribe whatever I demanded. My goal from the time I left home at age fourteen was to have a happy, loving family and a good life. I had no desire to brush over the cause of a problem and simply manage the effect, yet this seemed to be the focus of these professionals. As I came to terms with being rejected by traditional medicine, I began to explore naturopathic medicine.

While exploring and questioning and looking for the root cause of my problems, I had an extraordinary experience. As much as it got my attention and made me fully open my eyes and my mind for the first time, I did not begin to comprehend its significance until many years later. For years, I was afraid to speak of this event for fear I would find myself locked up in a mental hospital, as so often was the case for my dear mother.

The experience occurred in April 1990. Six months had passed since the diagnosis of my brain tumor. I was living daily with extreme pain.

One afternoon as I was driving west toward the mountains for a business appointment, I experienced a time of intense clarity. It was a clear day with only a few white, fluffy clouds in the sky. It seemed to me that at that moment the sky got brighter, the mountains were crisp, and everything looked sharp and crystal clear. In an instant, I could see out of both eyes and the pain in my head was gone. This happened at the exact moment that I heard a voice say to me that my mother was not the problem or the cause of my pain; rather, it was my expectations of how I wanted her to be. In those insightful seconds, I also realized that she must have been in a lot of pain herself to have abused and neglected her children. I realized that she was not a monster; she was angry, reactive, and unaware of how much her words hurt or how much I needed to have her show me that she loved me.

All this took less than a minute, but it felt as if time stood still. I was clear-headed, healthy, strong, and confident for the first time, and it was remarkable! I felt compassion for my mother instead of hate and anger. My next medical test showed that the tumor was gone. The doctors and specialists could not explain why this occurred. They said that possibly I had suffered from a swelling of the brain, not a foreign growth.

That was more than twenty years ago and I never had the surgery. I was left with a severe case of vertigo, which prevented me from moving too quickly; I couldn't swim, walk fast, turn left too quickly, or have stripes or dots move by my right side. I was unable to drive for several months or to read a book if my eyes needed to scan from left to right. I took pills to keep my stomach from rejecting food every time I got dizzy or lost my balance. The neurologist told me I needed to stay still, which meant I couldn't ride the stationary bike at the gym, swim, drive, or run.

I recall asking him if I was allowed to get up to turn on the TV or if I was limited to using the remote. I was horrified. I was never a gal who went to the gym until this doctor listed his rules. I took this as a challenge and I joined a gym, learned to read upside down, swam on my back, rode the stationary bike, and even took skiing lessons the next winter. I took public transit and got on with my life. I still see the expressions on the faces of passengers who shared the train as I read books upside down. In only a few months, I was able to drive and get on with my life. To this day, I still need to be careful not to move too fast to the left, but I never fall or lose my balance. This was my first experience in listening to my intuition instead of the advice of professionals. The limiting words, spoken with such conviction by this neurologist, changed my life. I continued taking the prescribed drugs and visited the hospital regularly to have my heart arrhythmia monitored and for my time on the breathing machine. My collection of prescriptions was growing as each year passed.

I did not question the direction and advice of the medical doctors. During this time I was diagnosed with 114 environmental allergies and later with 225 food allergies. I was aware that I was getting worse, not better, and was curious about why this was the case when I was following the care of the doctors. I was told that I would require an oxygen tank by the time I was forty!

I was horrified. I did not drink, smoke, or do drugs. I ate foods on the approved Canada Food Guide list; I cooked my meals from scratch and lived a quiet life. How could this be happening to me at such a young age? I was determined to figure out why my body was rejecting everything. I couldn't be near flowers, eat rice, or enjoy foods of almost any kind. Even lettuce and onions could cause an attack. I was taking so many drugs for my asthma and anxiety attacks that I felt overwhelmed. Trying to breathe and finding food that I could eat was extremely difficult. I avoided products that contained chemicals, and though I saw some improvement, I was still gaining weight each year. I recall vividly being told by a doctor that I was undisciplined and in denial about what I was eating and that was why I was fat. She said she would not take me as a patient, since I was tagged in the computer as someone shopping for doctors and she wanted nothing to do with my kind. With this, I accepted that there was no one to turn to for help. Nobody else was experiencing such rejection by the body, so there were no support groups. I was exhausted and scared and felt alone. Knowing I was on my own left me feeling isolated and frightened for my life. I was confused and didn't know which way to turn, since I was convinced that I was undeserving of anything.

One day in 1993, I heard a speaker talk about how children will attach pain and fear to objects instead of their parents. The speaker said this is a coping mechanism for children in abusive situations because they are unable to attach blame to a parent when they are very young.

Having given this some thought, I realized that my three biggest allergies to flowers were to roses, lilacs, and mums. My mother's name is Rose, her favorite flowers are lilacs, and she grew mums whenever she had a garden. She said mums kept the bugs away. I began to question if this was why I was allergic to these flowers. Desiring to test this possibility, I began walking to the park every day. At times I had to crawl or stop and sit when I was near flowers, since my energy would drop, making my legs so weak that they could not support me. As I spent time in the park, I would say to myself that I wasn't angry at the flowers, and I would acknowledge that we are made of the same stuff, since we are all creations of the great universal source of life. I would say that it was my mother I was angry at, not nature. To my surprise, not long after doing this, I was at a house party one evening, and as I turned around I discovered a huge bunch of cut lilacs on a piano right behind me. Until then, I would have passed out if I was within three feet of a single lilac. I was impressed and began expanding this process to other items causing a reaction in me. I learned how to do kinetic testing (muscle testing) and used this process for selecting food, cleaning products, cosmetics, and personal care products. Today I am fine with most things. Chemicals are the worst, chlorine being my greatest remaining sensitivity. To this day, my tongue thickens, my lips feel like rubber, I can't think, and I get very cranky (to put it mildly), so I try to avoid chlorine. This is a challenge when I use public washrooms or travel.

I have since learned that many of the additives put in foods make us crave them and that the high amounts of sugar in everything, including our toothpaste, add to our resistance to burning fat. In addition, genetically modified foods are not regulated. To market a product as "natural," all that is required is one natural ingredient. In many products, water is the natural ingredient. Some consider me a fanatic, and others think I live a deprived existence. I do not drink coffee, juice, pop, or much alcohol. I drink well water, have no chemicals inside or outside of my home, and use no window treatments or fire retardants if possible. Solid oak floors and solid wood or leather furniture keep me healthy and vibrant as I approach sixty.

People often comment that I look much younger, and even the Wii game tags my biological age at twenty years below my chronological age. I do not crave things that are not good for me; in fact, I have no cravings at all. I know that when I buy into an ad and try a product that promises delight, I will leave my satisfied state and quickly feel a need for more sugar, salt, or crunch. When this temptation happens, I am able to bring experiences to my awareness that lead me back to making healthy choices for my body, mind, and spirit.

This is because I have reprogrammed my ego mind. The information stored in these files regarding satisfying and pleasurable food is aligned with choices that keep my body, mind, and spirit at their best. We must make healthy choices in all facets of life, including the food we eat, the supplements and drugs we take, the things we drink, our exercise routines, the professionals we trust, and our environments at work and at home.

The companies promising a slimmer you, a younger you, a more vibrant you, depend on your purchases to survive. Advertising gurus do not have your best health in mind. You are a statistic, a clearly categorized being with biology that can be altered to induce cravings. All this negative data grabs your awareness, and soon you believe that you need these products to be healthy.

Do your homework and listen to your body as you explore which products work for you and which ones hook you into wanting more. I have learned that the things we crave are often the ones that are not good for us. Give that some thought and watch for changes in your energy, your body, your cognitive abilities, and your temperament, since foods, drinks, drugs, and chemicals can have a subtle impact.

Stop believing that it is normal to have pain in your joints as you get older or that your vision will fade, that you won't have as much energy, or it that is difficult to have a strong and flexible body. These mind viruses, which Richard Brodie calls memes, lead us to accept that false beliefs ingrained in our culture are true. There is no reason for anyone not to be strong, healthy, and vibrant. The solution is simple and often excludes many of the products netting billions in profits each year.

The problem is that we blindly trust the promises that these products are good for us and underestimate the impact of big business and the drive to make billions of dollars. There is no law in the corporate world that human life must come first. We are too often the proverbial lab rats, the test subjects for products that are recalled once too many people, including children and the elderly, die or are harmed. Aspartame and DDT are two examples of products removed from public access after test subjects over decades proved that they cause harm. Give thought to what you eat, breathe, drink, taste, inhale, and put on your skin. Your body has to last you a lifetime!

In 1995, I put all the drugs I was taking, inhalers included, into a plastic tub and sealed it. My toughest challenge was getting through the withdrawal stage and refusing to use these drugs any longer. It didn't take long. That was roughly seventeen years ago, and for better than fifteen of those years, I have lived without needing an antibiotic, an inhaler, or any other medication.

I have a uniquely strong immune system that fights off those flus and colds to which we are all exposed. A few hours of a rocky tummy or a slight fever is all I suffer, since my body does what it is designed to do. I enjoy food and love to cook. I no longer live in fear of eating something that will attack me. It took much trial and error before I could trust that my body knows what is best and that I could rely on the signals. Just like anybody, I am affected by processed and genetically altered foods. The difference is that I know when I have eaten something that was not good, so I know not to do it again, at least not too often. You may be wondering if I have big turkey dinners at Thanksgiving, Easter, and Christmas. Yes, I do, with all the trimmings, and I love every bite!

When you love your body and allow yourself to be optimally healthy, you gain the freedom to enjoy all the pleasures life has to offer. For me, these pleasures no longer are dictated by marketing that prescribes which foods are satisfying or healthy. Instead, what brings me pleasure is enjoying healthy foods that I know are contributing to my optimum health. This is a reason to feel joy and to celebrate. The subliminal messages, the hypnotic factors that apply to health issues, are staggering in number. Set the volume on low when listening to these messages and tune into your body.

It is speaking to you when you have a headache, a pain in your back, knee, or neck. Brain fog and naps after eating are signs that your body is not doing well with your food choices.

Many years ago, a book by Louise Hay called *You Can Heal Your Life* became my body symptom bible. Each time I experienced a difficulty in my body, from a cramp in a toe to an earache to a cold sore on my lip, I would look up the cause in her book, and sure enough, when I applied the affirmation she suggested, the issue would resolve itself without prescribed drugs. I soon learned to recognize the signals my body was giving me. This book remains an essential item in my library.

Health is of utmost importance, Without it, life is limited and often painful. I challenge you to look beyond the surface and get to know what strengthens and supports your body. Don't wait until you are close to collapse or death before you are motivated to care for your body. We get one body. It can simply endure or it can flourish. The choice is yours. If you take these words to heart and want to shorten the process, the best program I have found for teaching people how to know their bodies is Dr. Jonny Bowden's "Unleash Your Thin" at www.naturalhealthsherpa.com. There are many programs to choose from; do your homework and find the one that is the right one for you. You must give priority to caring for your body, and no one else knows your body as intimately as you do.

EXTERNAL INFLUENCE TWO: WELLNESS

Wellness is a word favored by those advertising products and trying to sell us on health coaches, doctors, natural food stores, and seminars. Take note of how many shops and products use the word in their marketing materials, including the name of the company in many cases. This word appeals to our desire to make healthy choices, and the word also produces a feel-good sensation. We warm up to it because we all long to feel well. Take time to define what this word means for you and screen the products and services that use this word. Make sure that what you are choosing is in line with your needs and desires. Many great companies are using this word to get our attention, but just as many are using it to sell products or services without care for their harmful effects. We all love to have money, and key words like *wellness* attract money, since people will pay to feel well.

EXTERNAL INFLUENCE THREE: SELF-HELP AND PERSONAL DEVELOPMENT

This category is an interesting one. I began sorting out my life by devouring information in the self-help, personal development genre. I followed the recommendations and applied principles like "Feel the fear and do it anyway" and "Fake it till you make it." I found myself in debt and more confused than ever. After years of doing the assignments suggested in the many books I read and programs I attended, I was still overweight, unhealthy, struggling financially, and not only scared but now confused.

The possibility that my mother might be right, that I was a stupid woman, was becoming more plausible as I consistently failed to get the results I was seeking. I was confused about why these programs were not working for me when so many people appeared to be successful as a result of applying the information they learned. I did the homework and the exercises and followed the advice without deviating from or modifying the processes. I would have given up if I wasn't so convinced that it was all a matter of learning, searching, and finding the right answers. I could not accept that I was defective as a human being. I knew that I could think, speak, hear, see, walk, and talk, so all I needed to do was to identify what was blocking me from getting the results I desired. I could not give up, since I didn't want a life of feeling useless and being thought of as heartless. This would confirm my mother's view of me.

As I persisted in exploring who I was, determined to discover why I was so stuck, I expanded the scope of my exploration to include spirituality. With this new information, I began to wonder if I brought bad karma with me when my spirit reincarnated into my body. I had no idea if I believed in reincarnation, but I knew that I had done nothing in this lifetime to justify the life I had so far, so I thought it was worth exploring whether my many challenges were indeed due to karma. I was close to forty, in poor health, and had no sense of self-worth, no sense of direction, and no sense of belonging. I was physically weak, discouraged, filled with fear. My fears increased because it seemed evident that if thousands of volumes of self-help information were not working and my financial and physical conditions were deteriorating. At forty-two I was dealing with my second diagnosis of cancer. I had little hope of achieving my goal of a happy, peaceful life. The odds were not in my favor.

These were the thoughts held in my ego storage center at that time. When I was confused or feeling stuck, my awareness, brought to my attention by my ego mind, affirmed that I was crazy to think I could beat such odds or that I could outsmart the evidence that I was nothing but a loser. My ego reminded me that I needed to accept this, since nothing could change reality and no one, including my mother and siblings, cared about me.

I had quite a dramatic and narrow view of myself and my life, wouldn't you agree? Can you imagine where I would be today if I were not determined to find a way to live my life as a competent, lovable, caring, happy, and contributing human being? I am so grateful for the light that burned inside me, the drive that kept me believing that I was not the monster my mother had told me I was. I knew that if I broke the grip these words had on me, I could have a great life. I knew that I was on my own in sorting through all this and that if I gave up on my dreams, my life would never be the one I believed possible. I had no choice but to keep searching and asking questions. I could not accept that I was not worthy of love.

I gave my ego no consideration until recently, but when I did, my life changed. That moment was like looking into a kaleidoscope; pictures swirling in circles suddenly came into focus and the big picture was now crystal clear in every detail. I am writing this book because in all the reading I did and the courses I attended, there was no information on how we could completely change our programming. As I explored the spiritual side of life, I learned that beliefs were held at many levels in our subconscious and conscious awareness and that we could change this data by changing a belief. But this is not an easy task, and until I understood that our ego holds our awareness, our beliefs about who we are, I struggled with seeing only small changes, some permanent, some temporary. They seemed random, making it difficult to relax and know that the change I wanted in a belief was actually completed. I do not pretend to understand this ego relationship fully, nor to be an authority on the human ego.

The role of the ego is not given a lot of consideration when we evaluate what has an impact on the human experience. We know we have an ego, and we know that the human mind accepts or discards thoughts. Many spiritual teachings share the idea that the ego is separate from God, the universal source, or the higher power. I have studied the process of taming the gremlin within us, but never have I read anything about how to understand and work in unison with our ego. This was the information that transformed my life, allowing me to dance with my ego as an equal partner. No longer bombarded with illusions of inferiority or superiority, my thoughts are congruent with who I truly am. My only goal now is to be the best me I can and never to forget how easy it was to be limited by my own awareness.

For most of my life, I blamed my mother for the pain and fear I held in my heart and soul, the very essence of who I was. After all, her harsh words defined who I was. Her words created doubt, fear, and anxiety in me, and I held her accountable.

The truth is that it was these words, stored in my data bank under the definition of who I was, that caused the pain and fear. Yes, my mother said them, but it was my mind that accepted them as the truth and allowed them to be repeated every time I checked in with my ego to acquire data about who I was. I can't get back the time I lost with my mother while listening to my ego, but I can know better and make the best of what I have today. The greatest lesson I have learned is that living in the present is what matters. Yesterday is gone, tomorrow is yet to come, and the only time that I can be who I am, fully present and available, is in this moment. This is where I put my energy, and I pay close attention to my thoughts.

After twenty-plus years of studying spirituality and human nature, I have concluded that when we are born we have an ego mind and a soul (spirit mind). Our ego mind is like a sponge, soaking up everything to which it is exposed in our environment. This includes our culture, our home, and of course our parents and family. The ego is a blank slate when we are born, so it is able to absorb everything it encounters at an unimaginable rate. The spirit mind contains a sliver of our life source, and this sliver, which melds with our ego mind, is our connection to the wisdom of the great source. Some people call this source God, others the universe. There are many names for this source of life that the vast majority of people believe exists in some fashion. The two minds are forever separate, and each serves its purpose. The awareness of the ego mind shapes the person we present to the world. Our spiritual mind stays in the center of our being, available to support us and provide us with wisdom and encouragement. Neither the spirit mind nor the ego mind can determine what information our free will recognizes as true. That is a choice we have as human beings.

Free will is ours to do with as we choose. Neither our ego mind nor our spirit mind has the power to override our free fill. Free will is activated by giving our attention and energy to thoughts. We then act upon these thoughts and they manifest themselves in our lives. These manifestations can be positive or negative, depending on which thought we entertained. As I said, I have no science or evidence other than my life experiences to support these views, but since we are all made of the same stuff, I believe that if this process worked for me, it may work for others.

Before closing on this topic, I would like to share my view of the sliver of spirit that I believe is at our core. This is the visual I use as a simple way of wrapping my head around a big concept. I have concluded that this universal source, God, the great presence, or whatever it is called, is comparable to the vastness of the ocean. It is massive, extends farther than the eye can see, and contains more than the mind can fathom. It is not solid, yet it is present. Removing a bucket of water from the ocean does not deplete it; removing even dozens of buckets does not make a dent in this vast body of water. The water in the bucket is very much a part of the ocean, just like the water that remained in the ocean. The water in the bucket does not change until we freeze it, allow it to evaporate, add something to it, and so on.

We can see our life source as comparable to the ocean, bigger than we can imagine or comprehend, supremely intelligent and wise. The spirit in each of us is a sliver of this source, containing the wisdom of the source in smaller quantities, just like the bucket of water from the ocean. We have intelligence and wisdom in our sliver of spirit that are the same, only less powerful, as those qualities in our source—just as the water contained in a bucket does not have the same power as the ocean. How many people fear a bucket of water heading their way, yet prepare when warned of a pending hurricane or tsunami?

When we are born, our spirit is not a blank slate like our ego mind. We have access to both the ego mind and the spirit mind, and these two minds are one within us. Our free will allows us to make choices, including which of these mind sources we will unconsciously and consciously acknowledge. Again, there is no science or evidence to support these ideas, but once I figured this out and began taking the actions that I have shared with you, I gained health, balance, and freedom and was filled with joy and wonder. This is evidence enough for me, since I think all of us want to feel great, enjoy life, and know that we belong. When you are living as your genuine self, your spiritual self and your ego self are a team. Then you have no more doubt or negative thoughts about who you are. Life becomes simple and beautiful. You know that you can handle whatever comes your way and that you do not need to perform miracles to be worthy of love. You know that being who you are is enough and that this is all you were born to do.

The self-help, personal development genre is a great tool with much information to offer. Be selective about what you believe, in determining what works for you, and do not doubt your thoughts or intuition as you go through any process. Self-help writers and gurus share experiences that make us think and bring us hope and provide information that can change our awareness of who we are. They can also lead you to feel more trapped and confused and less worthy. When this is how you feel, your ego is affirming what you hold in your awareness as the truth for you and the information that you are buying into is propaganda, not the truth of who you are. Don't let your ego lead your life. Be aware that your ego can lead you away from the truth of who you are. So listen to the information you receive, the thoughts in your mind, and then decide which beliefs you will live by.

EXTERNAL INFLUENCE FOUR: SPIRITUALITY

This is one of my favorite topics and one that appears to captivate many of us. For twenty-plus years, I have been devouring information on angels, demons, witches, fairies, God, the universe, Buddha, Krishna, Christianity, and so on, and I am not alone on this quest for understanding. It seems that we all want to know if there is more to us than what we see and experience in our human form. We may have a similar curiosity about the possibility of aliens. Why is spirituality such an attention getter? What is it that we really want to know? Is it because we fear death or feel such a deep sense of wanting to belong, or is it simple curiosity about where we came from that drives us to search? The question of origin has been asked since the dawn of man. Man has spawned many religions, believing they have the answers, and throughout time, the masses have been drawn to religion as they strive to give meaning to their lives. Wars are fought over which religion is the right one. For centuries, people and countries have been divided over which religion should rule. This topic inspires passion for most of mankind. Even tribes living in the jungles worship their gods. The need to feel connected to something bigger has permeated every corner of this planet. For generations, human beings have searched far and wide and have theorized and pondered the possibilities. All this effort is focused on finding tangible and quantifiable evidence that there is a life source out there.

No one wants to feel insignificant, here for a short while and then gone forever. We all search for the answers to these questions because we want to believe we matter in life and after death. To this end, we focus on money in hope of leaving a legacy. We search relentlessly for our purpose, that one thing that will endorse our lives as having been worth living. We drink alcohol, do drugs, and turn to addictions to numb the pain of not knowing if we have taken care of the afterlife. We seek to fill a void that we feel so strongly. We want to be loved, to feel that we are enough; we want to feel that we are of value, that we are important in this life, and that we will not be forgotten when we die. This fear of living a life as someone insignificant adds to our fear of being lonely, lost, or forgotten. These fears are real to many people and motivate us to search for answers to our spiritual questions.

No religion provides the sense of belonging felt when we find that spark, that light at the core of our being, that sliver of spirit trying to get our attention. This shard of pure spirit is often buried under layers of negative information adopted as our belief about who we are. We have lost touch with the spirit in us as we search the world of logic and theories. This is the message the churches are trying to deliver, but many people are distracted from looking within themselves by the many external influences, including the message that we should not get too full of ourselves and presume that we have wisdom. We are drawn to the promise that we will have the life we long for now and in the afterlife if we find the right group to follow.

Any religion teaching that we must feel guilty or obligated, or that we must fear the higher power, is not for me, since it does not flow with my desire to feel confident, valued, and loved for who I am. I prefer to believe that the higher power, which I am adamantly convinced does exist and in which I place 100 percent of my faith and trust, is founded in loving each of us as who we are, without judgment or critique. I believe we are supported through our spirit, which is available at our core being, and that all we need to do is to communicate, ask, then listen to the wisdom within.

Our spirit knows that we are enough, that we are valuable, and that we are unconditionally loved. We can access that knowledge every time we quiet our minds and listen to the wisdom of our genuine self by connecting with the spirit within us. The irony is that instead of doing this, we are spending time and money seeking answers outside of ourselves, turning to the manifested world created by humans who are so busy searching for the mystical higher power outside of themselves that they have given little or no priority to finding a quiet moment to still their minds and listen.

As we quietly listen to our spirit, our soul, we will find that we feel energized, safe, secure, and valued. Our inner self, our spirit, is not negative or critical. For some, and for many first getting comfortable with meditating, it is common to doubt this internal voice or be uneasy with the sense of feeling wonderful, since this may seem foreign and unfamiliar. For some, this can be a disturbing or a frightening experience. Feeling that things are strange or uncomfortable is common when we are exposed to something new. Meditation is an exercise in quieting the mind and allowing yourself to hear the spaces between your thoughts. You are in complete control of your mind and cannot be influenced by any thought that is not in your ego mind or your spiritual mind, so you are safe. In this quiet space, you are able to hear and, in many cases, see yourself and your thoughts. This enables those skilled in meditation to heal themselves, to explore past lives, and to develop an intimate awareness of themselves. This is the express route to getting to know who you are at the center of your being and to selecting the information you want to remove from your ego data files.

In my early days of meditation, I would soak in a bubble bath to relax my body and put on quiet instrumental music or sounds of nature to help me focus my mind on being still. In the beginning, I kept a pad of paper nearby, since I needed to write down the thoughts that dominated my mind when I was trying to quiet it. Putting things down on paper worked well for me, and soon I had some interesting to-do lists and ideas to explore as a result. I developed a habit of keeping a journal and making lists before going to bed. Be patient with yourself if meditating is a new experience. It is important to respect your needs in this process. There is no race, no finish line, so relax and enjoy playing with ideas and finding ways to still your mind.

Like anything else, learning to meditate takes practice and some getting used to, but I can assure you that you will be better for doing it. After more than twenty years of meditating, I can attest to the value of incorporating this practice into your life. When I was too busy and too distracted by life to find time to meditate, my health failed, I was conned and swindled by self-serving people whom I trusted, my business was sabotaged, and I felt lost and filled with fear. My ego was firing data at me fast and hard as I struggled with the possibility that I was worthless, helpless, and could never be enough. I could write a book on the negative data held in my ego. It would be a story of tragedy, drama, and heartache—possibly a best seller, since many people are drawn to hard-luck stories that affirm they are not alone in experiencing tough lives.

We are creatures of habit and comfort, which is why external influences are so plentiful. Marketing experts count on this when they develop their plans. Spirituality has also become big business, so keep your antenna up, your senses honed, and trust the wisdom within you as you search for answers.

Instead of taking inventory of all that can go wrong and giving thought and energy to preparing for the worst, we should change gears and take charge of the data that we are inputting into our awareness. Listening to stories of survival only supports the belief that we are victims. This feeds our fear that such things could happen to us. This negative support is so common that it is not easily recognized for what it is.

This brings to mind a story that I heard on an investigative news program. I don't recall the name of the program or the name of the woman involved, since I popped in while the show was in progress, but what I did catch was disturbing. The woman, in her late thirties and severely overweight to the point that she could not leave her home easily, had been the victim of a man who kidnapped her when she was a young child and held her captive in a basement for several years. She was found at age twelve and freed from this prison. The program focused on how she felt about her abductor being up for parole. He was interviewed from his jail cell. What I found interesting was that years after the kidnapping, she blamed him for her obesity, for being trapped in her apartment, and for fearing to do something with her life. I was even more surprised at the support this young woman was getting from therapists, the media, and family members. They agreed that she was right to blame this man for destroying her life and to resolve to remain in pain. In doing so, they helped keep her imprisoned by her past.

I am in no way saying that her kidnapper should be out on parole or that she should just forgive and forget. However, this event occurred more than twenty years earlier. Why weren't the people rallying around this frightened woman encouraging her to grow past this horrific experience instead of helping her affirm that she was a victim?

She was kept a prisoner by her fears, not by the event or by her abductor. She was no longer in danger, but she had not come to terms with the impact of post-traumatic stress on her life. I could not understand why this was not the direction the people supporting her were taking. My heart went out to her. I wanted to scream out that she was not a victim. She was more than capable of moving past this event and having a great life, but first she needed to let go of all the attention that being a victim was getting her. She did not need the people around her to remind her that she had the right to feel bad, beaten, and frightened. She needed to be surrounded with people who believed she could move past this. The injustice being done had nothing to do with her kidnapper; those she trusted to help her did the real injustice. She needed to be loved and seen as a strong, capable woman, not as the poster child for how another human being can destroy a life. She was only in her late thirties and had her whole life ahead of her.

Her kidnapper had his own cross to bear, but that was none of her concern after twenty years. She was committed to reliving her experience every day as she had for the past twenty years. She could not undo what was done, but she could find the beautiful woman buried beneath a mountain of fear, get out of that apartment, and discover that the world would embrace her for doing so. I hope this story makes you think about how easy, how common, it is to find support for those bad days, tough experiences, and disappointments.

We all have difficult experiences; that is not going to change. The question is, will we let these define us or will we dust ourselves off and move on? Do not allow the support team around you to reinforce the negatives in your life. This can be difficult because when we are down we are attracted to those who agree that our plight is real. Be selective. Feel the experience and then move on.

The world is full of heroes. They are on every street in every town and city in the world. Look at 9-11 and the people who came together, not out of pity but out of a desire to help. The same goes for Hurricane Katrina, for the tsunami that hit Japan, or for many other disasters. People care a lot, and they feel valued when they contribute. When catastrophes happen, we see the best in people. This reflects our underlying desire to contribute. We want to feel great about ourselves every day, to know that we made a difference and helped in whatever way we could. This is our spirit in action. This is the feeling you want to encourage, not the fear that too often enters our awareness.

Admiring someone for having the courage to keep going despite obstacles is one thing, but commiserating with the pain and suffering and feeling pity or sadness for the victim only adds to the negative data in the person's ego. When you face an obstacle, your ego will draw on that data and bring victim status to your awareness of who you are. You want your ego to bring you the awareness that you are strong, vibrant, and able to handle whatever adversity comes your way.

I don't think of myself as the survivor of a traumatic, dramatic life. I am grateful for the experiences I had in this life, since they forced me to ask who I am and if I am who I want to be. This helped me know who I am as a spiritual being. I feel that I am a spiritually aware human being who is not afraid to be who she genuinely is in her everyday world. You too can have this experience, but you must search for the answers within yourself. You must learn to trust who you are in your core being, and you must put faith in your inner guide and spirit.

Finding the time to go within and meditate is the key to this secret world. If you don't like the word *meditation*, call it thinking, contemplating, pondering, me time, anything that will allow you to fully relax, slow down the chatter in your mind, and feel your own presence.

I rarely let a day go by without meditating, even if it is for five minutes. On a great day, I will mediate for three or four hours. It is like an afternoon at a spa. I feel rejuvenated, calmer, at peace with my life, and ready to go another mile. After many years of resistance, fear, and questioning, I came to appreciate that I was connecting with my life source and that the little sliver of spirit within me is part of the great source of life that loves us all. Knowing this spirit is connecting me to the source of life brings me a serenity that is difficult to put into words.

> *Language ... has created the word loneliness to express the pain of being alone. And it has created the word solitude to express the glory of being alone.*
>
> —Paul Tillich

As you explore who you are, including your spiritual self, consider the meaning of words. Words like *love* are loaded with meanings. You might believe that a person is being harsh because he says he loves you and wants you to learn a lesson. Thus you might feel fear instead of warmth and comfort when you hear the word *love*. Another word subject to debate is *truth*. For some, truth is based on a judgment, whereas others see truth as an absolute with no gray area or perspective attached. Words like *commitment* and *real* are also subject to interpretation. Think about this as you pull information together. Be sure the words you choose to program into your ego mind hold the intent you desire. For example, if you are reminding yourself that you love yourself and your interpretation of love is "love hurts," you are saying that you have the right to hurt yourself. Give words heartfelt thought, since they are one of the subtler ways in which we sabotage our growth.

While on the topic of spirituality, I would also like to discuss the word *faith*. Faith is having a belief in something or someone without doubt or question. It is important to be aware that you can place your faith in only one thing at a time. For example, you cannot have fear and faith at the same time. You can put your faith in yourself or in a stranger, but not in both at the same time. We all have faith in something. This could be our government, our banks, our doctors, our God, our parents, or even the promises made in the advertising that we hear.

If your life is not one you are consciously choosing, you need to ask where you have placed your faith, since that faith is manifesting a world for you to live in. Only you can choose where you place your faith. Only you can live your life and walk in your shoes. If you put your faith in your internal spirit, you will learn to know and to trust yourself. You will find the answers to your questions with confidence. If you put your faith in the outer world, you will not receive those answers provided by your source. You will miss the boat. You cannot put your faith in two things at the same time. It is not possible. You cannot have fear and faith at the same time, yet fear dominates the people who relentlessly search for evidence of the higher power in which they place their faith. These people have placed their faith in whatever they fear.

Imagine what would happen if people put their faith in themselves and their genuine self and listened to the spirit within them. The dream of world peace could become a reality. Achieving it starts with each of us choosing where we put our faith. Is your faith in commercials, propaganda, and world leaders, or is it in your genuine self, which you know will never trick you, criticize you, lie to you, condemn you, leave you, or stop loving you?

This is an important question to answer, and for many it requires a leap of faith. The fears, the realities we are familiar with, are not easily dismissed or dismantled, making this question one that can take much inner reflection to answer. My faith in life's source is very strong, and that is why I have such faith in myself. I know who I am and am proud to be me. I sometimes refer to the source as God, the universe, or the great presence, and I respect that those who have faith in a higher power have many names for this source. It makes no difference to me what this source of life is called.

What matters is that we look within to find our personal access to this source and then place our faith within it. Even those who have not connected with the source, or who do not feel there is one, can find serenity by meditating, quieting the mind, and listening to those softly spoken thoughts. You do not need to believe in a source of any kind to have access to who you are. You are uniquely you, and nothing can change that, not even a world filled with negative thoughts or an ego that has stored these thoughts in your awareness. I hope that you find your genuine self during your time here in human form so you can live the joy and freedom that this brings.

EXTERNAL INFLUENCE FIVE: MONEY

Money is another big topic. We all agree that we need money to have any quality of life, right? Gotcha! This is not true and is in fact one of the big myths that we are being sold, one that our ego too often uses to measure our degree of success. We have attached many markers for success to money, and people have proven they will do anything for money. We have a distorted belief that money gives people power. Try this little experiment and decide for yourself.

EXERCISE EIGHT

Take a twenty-dollar bill and place it on a plate in the middle of your dining room table when you go to bed tonight. In the morning, when you wake up, make a list of all the things that twenty dollars did for you while you were sleeping.

Are you surprised that the money was still lying on the plate, just as you left it? Do you think if you gave it more time, perhaps another night, things might change? It is still sitting where you put it because it is paper! It has no power, no ability to multiply, shrink, or change without your assistance! You can invest it, spend it, share it, or save it, but none of these things will happen if you don't decide to make it do something.

Money has power only when people give it power. Can we agree that it is we who decide what to do with our money, that money will do nothing left on its own? From this moment forward, let's stop believing that people with money have power and see them simply as people with many pieces of ordinary, lifeless paper. You can support what they do with their money or not; the choice is yours. If they believe they hold power because they have wealth, that is their belief. When we agree with this belief, they are correct. They have power over all those who share that belief. They do not hold power over those who do not share this belief.

What about people without money? Are they powerless? It is true they have different choices from those with more money, but are they powerless, less than others, or worthless? Are they people without real value? How about Mother Teresa? Gandhi? Abraham Lincoln? This is an important point to explore, since this is as big an issue as spirituality when it comes to pushing emotional buttons in people. How many people have destroyed their lives due to greed and a focus on money because they believed money had the power to solve all their problems?

How many people live their lives centered around their bank accounts and paychecks? They can't seem to get enough money or enough of the things money can buy. Does this remind you of how addicts need a fix or a drink? Through the centuries, people have borrowed, stolen, and cheated and then blamed money for these actions. It has become acceptable and commonplace to create movies, stories, and therapies based on human beings' insatiable need for money. Many people kill for money. Why is a human life worth less than money? .

What happened to make us feel so dependent on money that we will harm, kill, cheat, steal, and do whatever it takes to get it? When did we decide that our identity is attached to money and the stuff it brings? We are so focused on money being the cause and solution to our troubles that we are like mice running around in a wheel, looking for a piece of food, running faster, eventually feeling exhausted and defeated, and giving up.

You may be thinking that I have gone over the edge. Let me assure you that I get it and agree that having money is a good thing. I enjoy my money and respect and am grateful for it, so I am not one of those who think we need to shed all our material things and live as paupers. I simply want to challenge your beliefs about money so you can gain a new perspective on it and see how addictive it can be.

Have you ever thought about people who win lotteries and become instant millionaires? How many of these winners find themselves broke again and feeling abused by friends and family? How many lottery winners learn that having money leads to even more problems than they had before? I recall a news report showing how a young teenage girl had lost her life because her family could not manage such a windfall. This family described winning the lottery as a curse. They lost friends and were bombarded by people seeking their help. They longed to return to their former modest lifestyle. One family member said that even if they gave back the money, they could never recover what they lost.

Why is this pattern of difficulty so dominant among lottery winners? If we know that this is so often the outcome, why do we keep lining up to buy our chance at the big prize? Do we believe we would never have such an experience, because we know better than others did? Do we feel our only hope of having money is to win it? Are we really making a statement about how much we wish we had a different life? If money is the solution, why doesn't winning lotteries worth millions solve people's problems? Once they have all this money, they will never have another worry, right?

So let's discard the belief that money is power and the solution to our problems and explore the reality of money.

First, let go of the belief that you are a successful someone only if you have money. As long as you are using the material things that money can buy as your measure of your worth, you are allowing yourself to be tempted and hypnotized by the people selling you houses, furnishings, food, vacations, vehicles, and fashion. You will never have enough stuff, since there will always be a new and improved model to upstage what you've got. The more you believe that your surroundings validate your worth, the further you are from knowing your genuine self.

I am not saying you cannot enjoy nice new things and be true to who you really are. I am saying that your motivation for having money and material things changes when you are living with your genuine self in charge. I live in a beautiful home, have horses, dogs, and cats, own more than one vehicle, and travel when I so desire. I am fond of beautiful clothes and jewelry just like any other woman. The difference is that these material things do not define who I am. They are like the icing on a cake, the sweet part of life. I no longer stress over schedules when I travel or worry about paying my taxes or buying tires for my car. I do not have a huge nest egg or an unlimited income. In fact, I have a modest but good middle-class income and I have debt, bills, and expenses just like everyone else. The difference is that I do not think about money and I do not consider it a measure of my worth. I appreciate what I receive and I am grateful that I can pay my bills and take care of myself, but I do not give any energy to worrying about how much money I have, need, or think I will need in the future. I give to charities as I choose. I am generous and I value my money. I do not take it for granted, since I have been homeless twice and once had to file bankruptcy. So I understand the stranglehold money can have on us.

I learned that the more money I made, the more bills and demands I had for my money. My responsibilities grew. I needed to learn how to invest and protect myself from those who could come after my money. A simple car accident could be cause for a lawsuit if you have an income above a certain level and become a target. Before long, you need people to help you manage your money, and then there is the question of what to do with it when you die. Money does not equal the freedom you might think if you are without money. I have made money, lost money, and lived without it, and I discovered that I was always me, no matter what my income or cash flow. I was able to be generous, even when my purse strings were tight, by giving of my time. I was able to eat well by cooking my own food instead of buying the packaged, ready-to-eat, processed foods that eventually harmed my health. I had friends, fun, laughs, and tears during all financial times.

In the end, I decided that I was wasting too much time and energy trying to figure out how much I needed to make, confirming that I was financially sound, and managing my money.

One day I let it all go. I decided to keep life simple and live within the budget of my income. I don't take vacations or buy gifts or furniture using credit. I save a little with each paycheck, and I'm grateful that I can pay my bills and live in such a wonderful home. Since that time, I have never fallen short of what I need to sustain my life. I do not consider money to be the reason I am successful. I believe my money flows because I am responsible, respectful, and value it. I never use phrases like "I can't afford that." Instead I say, "It is not in my budget." Saying you can't afford something is a statement of lack, whereas saying something is not in your budget means that you control the flow of your money. I never run short and I always have the money to get what I want.

I also learned many years ago that you can indeed live without money. It is not my preference, but I now know it is not as scary as people think. The fear is that if you have no money others will no longer value you, that they will see you as a lesser human being or as a loser. This comes back to what I said about how placing judgments on others also places judgments on ourselves.

I recall a conversation with my sister, who was the president of a food bank in the interior of British Columbia during the big fires of 2003. Entire towns were destroyed. She observed that before the fires people would volunteer their time and often donated food or money, commenting how sad it was that people could allow themselves to get to a place where they needed to use a food bank. She said she often felt bad for the families that were looked down on and considered less capable than those donating food or volunteering their time. She said the people who had made these comments were humbled as they stood in line for rations after the fires, shoulder to shoulder with those whom they earlier judged as not as important. Imagine the impact on your self-esteem when you believe that those who need handouts from a food bank are less than they should be. This translates to believing that you are not a capable person if you are unable to take care of yourself and need to ask for help.

If your earlier judgment of these people was that it was great that they had somewhere to get help while they rebuilt their lives, your self-esteem would not be harmed as you stood in line at the food bank. You would then feel grateful for the food bank instead of feeling ashamed or embarrassed that you were in need.

Money is just paper. It is a way to trade for items that bring us pleasure, that fill our needs, but it is not a measure of our worth or of our success. Circumstances can change without warning, such as the fires in British Columbia, and then we are faced with the reality of what we value.

Wealthy people have many income levels, and many people living as hermits in cabins in the woods and surviving off the land are loving every day and living life to the fullest. Take time to examine your beliefs about money, especially how much of a role it plays in identifying who you are. If you were stripped bare and all your belongings and money were taken from you never to be returned, who would you be? Could you love who you are? Would you feel confident that you could start again and do it in style? Would you know that what you lost was not of value, that you—not your position, career, money, or home—are the precious jewel in your life?

EXTERNAL INFLUENCE SIX: VACATIONS

We are consistently reminded that we need a break to stay healthy and well. We need to get away, and if we do not, we will be deprived, considered a workaholic, anal, uninteresting, and no fun—all because vacations are considered a marker of success!

Vacations are designed by the tourism industry so that we will take that trip at all costs. Financial stress too often results when people believe they must have a vacation that involves a getaway. How many people go over the top with the tension of preparing for a vacation, spend the entire time away thinking about their responsibilities back home, and then complain that the buildup of work that occurred while they were away made them wonder if the vacation was worth it?

I have done some traveling and love exploring other cultures and locations, especially those with beaches and palm trees. Knowing this is something I thoroughly enjoy, I have still managed to go for nine years without a vacation. I once went sixteen years without a vacation, yet I continued to be sane, successful, and content. Why was that?

During the years when I did not take vacations, my work occasionally took me to the tropics, since I taught classes on cruise ships for a couple of years. This was work, not down time. When I feel I need to rejuvenate or take a break, I find taking the time to meditate, to sit quietly, and to go within is what works best. Yes, sitting along the ocean or a stream in a picturesque setting adds to the majesty, but closing my eyes and envisioning these things has the same effect. I compare this to the new Wii games. Virtual reality, we call it. We can play tennis, golf, jog, or ride a bike all without leaving home, and we get the physical benefits as well. This is the same as visualizing yourself walking in the sand or rowing a boat.

Again, give thought to why you are convinced you need to get away to feel rested. I am not opposed to vacations. I am opposed to people being sold the idea that this is necessary. They feel deprived and fear that they are risking their health if they don't take regular vacations and then get into debt and suffer stress when they do. Taking a holiday at all costs conflicts with my belief that if an expenditure is not in the budget, it is not a positive action, but a negative action that comes with consequences.

I recall being in Hawaii when Canada 3000 went into receivership, stranding many passengers around the world, myself included. As I lined up at the airport to leave Maui, I saw the tears of parents who had no credit left to fly home, people in panic and fear over how they could get off the island. We were able to leave on the limited flights available through other airlines, but first we had to pay the airfare and wait for a refund, provided we had travel insurance. That was fine for those who had not stretched their financial limit to take this vacation. I was saddened as I watched people, including entire families and wedding parties, who were stranded, stressed, and helpless. If I could have flown them all home, I would have, but I did not have the means. The situation made me think about why so many people put themselves in a position of being stranded just to meet that expectation of a vacation.

EXTERNAL INFLUENCE SEVEN: RELATIONSHIPS

Here's another category that has been enshrouded by propaganda, too often leaving us confused and disappointed. We have been taught that we need a partner, that we won't be whole or have hope of living a full life if we do not mate! Add to this that until we meet our soul mate, we are just settling. That's a scary thought! No wonder there is so much fear and anxiety around relationships.

The propaganda surrounding us is relentless in providing images of happy couples, walking hand in hand on the beach after fifty years together, and families of happy kids (at least two), the perfect house, vehicles, and of course the dog. These families play together, stand behind each other, and never have bad hair days! The couples are modeled after Ken and Barbie and they have perfect lives in every way. We learn through this propaganda that when we meet our soul mate life will be perfect; we will desire each other as if we were animals, uncontrolled and still passionate for each other after fifty years together. Our passion will be more than we imagined and will last a lifetime, and if it doesn't there is something wrong with us.

Then there are all the rules that determine the right partner. These rules require our soul mate to be the right race, sex, age, and height and have the right religion, hair color, intelligence, social status, income level, temperament, style, and more. Wow! Who made these rules and why? They sure do limit the possibilities for whom we can choose to be our partner! With the constant worldwide propaganda supporting these rules as if they were cast in stone, it's a wonder people find anyone with whom they can build a relationship. People feel confusion or attraction and want this to be love. Then they follow the rules of dating, move in together, and marry before they know who they are or what they need or want. They often spend borrowed dollars to celebrate their wedding day, starting their new life together with the stress of debt. They add to this by buying a house, because that biological clock is ticking and they need children and a dog. To keep up with the Joneses, they need to work two or more jobs, they rarely see one another, and the kids are in every group imaginable so that they are not deprived or burdened with poor self-esteem because they have few opportunities. After all, they deserve the best, and so do their parents.

Somehow we have concluded that the best is measured in material things, including the ideal career, relationships, and lifestyle. As the demand to appear like the perfect family wears on each person, everyone does whatever it takes to prevent the others from seeing what is really happening. Parents and children often feel exhausted, worried, and possibly embarrassed, confused, and frustrated even though they have followed all the rules. They are often so tired, so distracted with all the confusion, that they no longer remember or know what would make them happy, content, or complete. Why is it that so many people no longer know what would make them happy? How many couples have babies or buy houses in hopes of putting that spark back in their relationship? We all seek that spark, that rush we felt when we first met a romantic partner. We are convinced that when this dies or changes there is something wrong. Isn't this one of those rules? How many turn to drugs, relationships outside of marriage, alcohol, counseling, therapy, or suicide or simply run away? So why are there so many rules and so much propaganda concerning relationships? I haven't even touched on work relationships and friendships, but we can see that there are a lot of negative messages that make this an overwhelming topic to consider.

Much information, support, and attention are given to partner relationships and little or none to knowing who we are before we begin to seek our life partner. In fact, when people say they are walking away from their lives so they can find themselves, the people around them are often close to hitting the panic button. We even hire teams of people to intervene and bring them back to their senses.

Our culture does not value or support finding out who you are, searching for your inner truth, your genuine self. Too often this notion of finding oneself is considered something best discouraged or stopped! Is this because when you find your genuine self you are no longer hypnotized by propaganda? Is this because people have so much fear of what they do not know that they are afraid for you? People may fear you have gone over the edge when you are stepping back and looking at yourself with an open mind and an open heart. It is important to acknowledge that they are genuinely concerned for you. Talk to them about their concerns and share what you are doing and why it is important for you. Be clear that you value their opinion and ask that they respect that in the end you will make the choices that are best for you. Assure them that you are acting not out of disrespect but out of a desire to feel good about who you are.

When we are looking for a partner, a boss, or a friend through the filters of propaganda and rules, our focus is not on the person or on ourselves, but on whether someone measures up to the expectations that we have been taught. I learned this lesson with my expectation that my mother should be warm and comforting. She should have tucked me in at night with a gentle kiss on the forehead, and she should have wrapped her arms around me when I was scared. I wanted a fairy tale mother who wore dresses with aprons tied with perfect bows, who danced while cleaning with her feather duster. For close to forty years, I was angry at her because she didn't do these things and was not my fairy tale mother. The worst part was that as I grew to adulthood this fantasy of a fairy tale mother did not diminish. In fact, it was supported by my ego and by everyone I spoke to, affirming that a mother should be caring and loving and protective of her child.

When I was all of twenty-one. I was raped at knifepoint in my home in the middle of the night. After being discharged from the hospital, I went to my mother's home, expecting her to wrap her arms around me and make me feel safe. As I cried, she sat on the bed next to me and slapped my face, telling me to stop crying, that it was over so there was no need to cry and that my problem was that I was always feeling sorry for myself. I was so deeply hurt that I left Vancouver and vowed never to go back or to see her again. This was the event that my ego would retrieve from my data bank and bring to my attention for me to use as evidence that I was abused and neglected as a child and that my mother was heartless. I allowed my ego to collect as much evidence as possible to support this belief, using everything she did and every conversation I had with her. My database added reasons to hold on to the anger, the resentment, and the pain that I felt until the day I heard those words while driving in my car and the tumor in my brain disappeared. At that moment, I got it. I was punishing myself by holding on to all this pain and expectation.

My mother is who she is, and being angry, resentful, and judgmental of her was only harming me. I realized that my anger did not produce any changes in her. Eventually I saw that her angry words were not intended to be malicious or harmful. She was a reacting to something going on in her mind and in her heart, and understanding this was the first step to having a real relationship with my mother, a relationship without all the pain.

People often ask me if I forgave her. My answer is, there is nothing to forgive; she was only being who she was, and I was the one holding this as pain and viewing each action as an attack on me. She did nothing other than to be who she was. What is there to forgive? I am not her judge, her jury, or her keeper. That is between her and her source. I see her as a woman who has endured much pain and who lives in fear, and this is a very sad and scary place to be, so I hope I do not add any more pain to her life.

I understand how the propaganda of this world supported my anger, pain, and confusion, and I am always surprised at the reactions of people when they discover I have no resentment or anger toward my mother. In fact, I love and admire the courage it took for her to hang in there, to keep going even with all the abuse and neglect she endured. When she could, she worked hard-labor jobs that paid minimum wage. She did not drink, party, or abandon her responsibilities as a mother. She was hospitalized many times, and we were then taken to shelters or to stay with family. When she returned, she went back to work and did the best she could. Many times we lived in places that were abandoned and condemned, since she could not pay rent. My father would gamble or drink away the money she made, and we would be on the move again. She loved him and all of us, and she did the best she could, even with poor health.

Yes, my mother was angry and said hurtful things, and that isn't a good for any child, but as far as her being a heartless monster, the truth is quite the opposite. She was a woman with an eighth-grade education, no money, no support, and an addict for a husband, and she did all she could the best she could. She had five children, myself the oldest. She didn't stand up to my father without getting beaten for it. Her life was not about being selfish or uncaring. Her life was about survival, about doing all she could to keep food on the table and a roof over her kids. She could not cope and lived her life reacting to whatever came up the best way she could. Her constant warnings about not expecting too much out of life, men, the government, or the education system were her way of preparing me so I did not endure the disappointment she lived. She never spoke these words intending to deprive me of having a great, loving life; yet the propaganda of the world supported that negative data, reinforcing those limiting words that were implanted into my ego database when I was a child. These remained in my awareness well into my fifties. I now know it was my own awareness of who I thought I was that created the limited, painful, and confused life that I was living. My adult experiences were not the fault of my mother or father. I was setting myself up for disappointment after disappointment by believing the data brought forward by my ego thoughts. My parents and my history started the programming, but it was I who chose to continue to hold this information as true.

There is only one relationship that will bring you comfort, joy, peace, and security, and that is knowing yourself and living as the genuine you. When you are living in harmony with your authentic self, the human experience flows even on those sideways days. The people you attract are amazing, kind, and gentle. Those who don't agree with you or who think you are strange move on to find those who measure up to their expectations. As far as a life partner or mate, there is no longer competition, worry, or a sense of needing to fill a void, which means when that right partner comes along, the relationship enhances each life in the partnership. It can't get better than that!

> *Your task is not to seek love, but to seek*
> *and find all the barriers within yourself*
> *that you have built against it.*
>
> —Rummi

EXTERNAL INFLUENCE EIGHT: FINDING YOUR PURPOSE AND YOUR PASSION

This is the latest buzz topic in the world of marketing and making money. We are told that we cannot have peace, happiness, or success until we find our purpose and our passion. The propaganda surrounding this topic separates us from who we are, encouraging us to believe the answers are somewhere outside of ourselves and discouraging us from going within to discover who we genuinely are. Be aware of the information in this category and be selective about the direction in which it takes you. Trust that you can find your passion by doing more of what you love, adding these activities to your day as outlined in exercise five. Your purpose is to be the best you that you can be. Trust yourself to make great choices, to be kind, caring, and loving to yourself, your friends, your family, and your community and to reprogram your ego to bring your genuine passions and beliefs into your awareness.

EXTERNAL INFLUENCE NINE: SHOPPING, GAMBLING, AND SOCIALIZING FROM YOUR CHAIR

External influences are no longer something you can turn off or shut out by turning off the radio or the television. We shop, play games, gamble, search for information and services, and even socialize and date over the Internet. The Internet marketing gurus are using the Web to spread familiar propaganda, and sadly it is impossible to avoid or ignore. Even our phones are wirelessly connecting us. I get texts with links that instantly connect me to travel information or literature that I might find interesting. With Facebook, LinkedIn, Twitter, and YouTube, to name only a few, we are communicating at the speed of light worldwide with the click of a button. Knowing how these messages make you feel, change your energy, and affect your awareness is of critical importance. Don't be blinded by these subliminal messages. Keep your senses alert and your mind clear. Choose which messages you will accept as being good for you and block the rest. This is why computers come with a delete button and TV sets come with a channel changer and an off switch.

EXTERNAL INFLUENCE TEN: PAST LIVES

(Note to readers: I believe that we have lived many lives and that our soul—that sliver of pure spirit—is reborn. I respect that you might not share this belief.)

I have added past lives to this chapter on external influences because I believe that for many who have struggled with mysterious pain or who have felt an energy that they can't seem to explain, it is possible that these are memories from a past life that have been carried into the body via the soul connection (sliver of spirit). These past life memories can be hard to identify, making it difficult to clear or to resolve them. It may be necessary to seek the expert assistance of a therapist who does past-life regression therapy.

There is evidence that people can bring information with them from past lives that is harming them in this life. Often past-life regression therapy is required to resolve these issues, so do not rule out this possibility. If you are not seeing the results you expect from applying the exercises openly, mindfully, and with complete honesty, consider past-life regression as a process to clear these negative thoughts.

I suggest that this is something to consider based on my own experience. For most of my life, I had a morbid fear of fire. Even striking a match was not possible. I was so afraid of that tiny flame that I would freeze, panic, and run. It was a strange reaction, and I had a problem even lighting candles on my children's birthday cakes. I needed to psych myself up and assure myself I could do it. I knew this was strange, and I attributed this phobia to having endured two house fires when I was a child. My fear of fire was becoming an obsession, but I had no idea what to do about it.

As I learned to meditate and got good at going deep within myself, I developed an ability to go back in time and explore my life, making adjustments to things distorted in my present life. I decided to bring my dread of fire into a meditation, to the core within myself that connects with my spirit. In my meditative state, I traveled back to the days when people accused of witchcraft were burned at the stake. I felt the heat of the fire and the sadness, the physical surrender to the heat and the pain as my dress, my legs, and my torso burned. I was awake and alert as these flames enveloped my body and I cried for help.

Since this experience, I have had no resistance to lighting a match, building a campfire, lighting candles, and enjoying the light from the flames as it dances around me. The meditation that took me back to a past life changed my body response in this life, the one I am focused on now. The past is the past and it brings us information on how to do better. We can do only what we know and respond with what we know. The rest is yet to be explored. I have gone back into many lives and observed patterns that brought me clarity and insight. This has added to my confidence that we are connected to our spirit in the core of our being and that our spirit never dies. It is our soul, our light, our connection to the source, that is continuously, quietly, and gently loving us even though we may not be listening to it or aware of its existence within us.

The external influences I have touched on here could each warrant a book. There is so much more to be said about how they affect our lives. To sum up, external influences are those things that affect us from the outside—data coming from many sources, attuned to the basic programs and fears to which our ego mind responds. As you look around you, note how many people believe that someone or something is to blame for their life challenges. For example, how many blame the change in the economy for the financial struggles they have faced over the past few years? It is acceptable to blame the economy, lack of opportunities, karma, our past, genetics, money, religions, doctors, educators, cultural beliefs, and obligations to parents or employers. Do these provide justification for why our lives are not as we desire them to be?

All these explanations give us permission to deny our core self exists and block us from having the experiences we desire. Take responsibility for the thoughts you are allowing in your mind, and if they don't make sense in the context of experiences you have had in this life, explore past lives. Taking responsibility for our own life is a scary thought, especially if life has been a series of painful events. The bright spot is that the sooner you look to yourself for the answers, the sooner the pain will disappear and you will feel the freedom, joy, and grandness of the life you were meant to experience.

I hope you will identify these external influences to provide insight as you filter through the information flow, recognize how much negative data is entering your ego mind, and commit to diligently screening out what you do not want defining you. Understanding that the negative information surrounding you through propaganda is not always in your best interests will go a long way in assisting you to taking responsibility for yourself. I am not an alarmist nor am I a skeptic or a pessimist. Quite the opposite. I am aware of the good, the bad, and the ugly, but I also know the joy, the peace, and the freedom available to all human beings when they choose to be who they are. It is up to each of us to choose what we believe about who we are, knowing that when we find our true self, life will flow, our mind will calm, our body will relax, and our spirit will soar.

It ain't what they call you; it's what you answer to.

—W. C. Fields

Chapter 11

INTERNAL INFLUENCES

*If you hear a voice within you say, "You
cannot paint," then by all means paint,
and that voice will be silenced.*

—Vincent van Gogh

*A*ware of the smorgasbord of information available in the world,
we are now equipped to consider the impact these messages
have on our lives. To make informed choices in accepting the truth
of who we are, we first need to take an inventory of our internal
influences—the external influences that have become the thoughts
and beliefs we are acting on. Our awareness is the culmination of all
the thoughts and beliefs that we live by. It is who we think we are,
based on what we believe to be true about ourselves.

Many external influences are negative and can limit and block
people from realizing their potential. When we observe these with

an open mind and in combination with internal influences, we begin to see the whole picture and can redefine who we are and reprogram our ego data. As we observe our life, do we feel happy, content, and enthusiastic or are we bored, confused, and just putting in time waiting for something to change? With these observations, we can identify what we want to keep and what we want to change.

When I encounter someone who has been defined as having a big ego or as someone who is full of himself, I consider the possibility that he may be running as fast as he can, afraid to let his guard down for fear of what others will think of him. These are people who have attached all their personal value to the outer markings of success, accepting that the external world has defined who they are. Because they have no time to stop, to feel, or to appreciate what they contribute or to know what is in their heart and spirit, they do not see anything but what the external world expects of them. Then there are those robotically going through life, unengaged in what they are doing, following the flow, not rocking the boat or stepping out of line.

People who are not confidently expressing from their genuine self are giving so much energy to hiding who they are that they are often viewed as having a big ego and being full of themselves. On the other side of the scale are those I lovingly call chameleon people. They do not want to be seen and prefer to blend in. The reasons for this behavior don't matter. The fact is that they may be missing the peace, contentment, and happiness that life brings to those who are willing to be who they were born to be, as opposed to being who they think they should be or need to be—or who believe they have no choices.

When we face the truth about how internal influences are affecting our life experience, we begin to release ourselves from feeling oppressed, chained to the limitations of our experiences.

The bars that keep us in prison are chosen and defended by our ego. These bars sentence us to live in fear, feeling that we do not matter and can never be loved or feel joyful, peaceful, free, and content. Too often people spend a lifetime wondering if they will ever be enough.

These are the outer effects that result when our internal beliefs, stored in our ego awareness of ourselves, are based on negative and false thoughts. If we could look at each bar that we have chosen to build our personal jail cell and see the belief that is the foundation for that bar, what would our beliefs be? Many base their beliefs on fear of some kind. It might be a fear of loneliness, of losing someone or something, of never finding love or being loved, of never measuring up or of being enough. It might be a fear that people discover you are a fake, and with this comes the fear that you will lose everything, that your life is a house of cards. Add to this the fear that others will laugh at you or find you of no value, a fear that you are worthless, that you are a disappointment, that no one will understand you, and a fear that if you follow your dreams you will be labeled as someone living in a fantasy. As human beings, it is our nature to want to belong, to be part of the crowd. We are social beings and this can make the fear of being segregated, pushed aside, dismissed, or abandoned intimidating to consider, never mind to experience.

With so many fears to choose from, it is no wonder that people feel disheartened and hopeless. The designers of the propaganda that I mentioned in the previous chapter capitalize on knowing that people will embrace these messages and not even give them a second thought. The vast majority of negative messages are designed to affirm that these fears are real, that they are bigger than we are, and that we need to respect them. The bars that imprison us have an impact on the lives we live. These bars are the internal influences firmly imprinted in our beliefs. These beliefs are held in our personal database, and these are the thoughts that we act on when our ego brings us the data we request when questioning who we are.

In this chapter, my goal is to demonstrate how I was trapped by the bars I created, imprisoning me with the limited beliefs that I accepted as my truth for many years, and how these limiting beliefs produced the many challenges and lessons I experienced over the past forty years.

My life transformed instantly when I realized that I was putting my faith in the data I had unknowingly allowed to be programmed into my ego's data bank more frequently than putting my trust in my spiritually based genuine self. I was shocked when I understood with such clarity that it was my ego self that defined me as worthless, foolish, gullible, and unwanted. It was my ego that told me I was not good enough, smart enough, beautiful enough, or capable enough.

With this new insight, I became acutely aware that my ego held no positive descriptions of who I was. At first, when this shift occurred, I felt out of sorts, restless, agitated, lost, and frightened. I felt as if I had been kicked out of the nest, pushed so far from my comfort zone that I didn't know how to respond, think, feel, or behave. I had no sense of direction. I didn't know where to begin now that I understood how much power I had given my ego over my life. For the first few days, I slept more than ever. I was tired, and sleeping seemed to be the one thing I was sure I could do. I felt as if I were in a strange place, and even my body seemed different somehow. This sense of being different lasted for a couple of weeks

I spent time outdoors, sitting still and meditating, staring out into the horizon, aware that I felt full and empty at the same time. I was so peaceful, so content. There was no anxiety or emptiness in my body, mind, or spirit. I felt as if the world was my playground and all I had to do was decide what game to play. Nothing felt the same. I was not afraid anymore. I knew that I was enough and that I was wanted. I also knew that it was my ego telling me for all those years that I was not wanted, not good enough, the ugly duckling, too fat, a poor judge of character, and someone who would never be loved. I could see that each time I had a plan or an idea my ego mind would bring up old thoughts, providing the evidence with which I built my prison bars, restricting my world one limiting belief at a time.

I will never again allow my ego to be programmed with such negative, debilitating thoughts about who I am. My hope is that this book will inspire others to free themselves and join those of us who live life fully, enlightened and free. All human beings have the ability to free themselves from the limitations they have accepted and to be who they genuinely are. Attaining the place where you know who you are, and living as who you know yourself to be, is what we call ecstasy.

A statement in *The Shack*, a book by William Paul Young, was a light-bulb moment for me. He wrote, "Most birds were created to fly. Being grounded for them is a limitation within their ability to fly, not the other way around. Living unloved is like clipping a bird's wings and removing its ability to fly."

When I woke up and realized my truth, I was amazed to look back over forty years and see how many opportunities I missed because I was giving my attention to the thoughts of my ego mind. My ego had clipped my wings. I believed the limiting thoughts were real for me. These words from *The Shack* snapped me out of the daze of these limitations, and it became clear that I could soar if I accepted that it was possible.

EXERCISE NINE

Reading the following excerpts from my history, look for the patterns that resulted because I thought that my wings had been clipped; identify the thoughts that became bars keeping me within the boundaries of my personal limitations. These thoughts are not always easy to identify, since the propaganda and mind viruses in which we are immersed create an illusion that we too frequently perceive to be real. There are many such thoughts, some subtle, others obvious as I look back. When we are enmeshed in the events of life, things are not always obvious, so do not feel discouraged if you see any of these patterns in your life. The good news is that once you see them, you can address them appropriately. As I share this story, observe the negative thoughts that I have noted in italics. These are examples of limited thinking that was the cause behind the effect. Making this list and noting these limiting thoughts will help you develop the skill of exploring your experiences. It is always easier to see what others do wrong or what they could have done better. Use this story to develop the skills of being alert to negative thoughts and observing the patterns in your own thinking and life experiences.

This is the story of how a company came to be successful with Bernice M. Winter, founder and current CEO, at the helm.

It all began back in 1992–93. After many months of recuperating from the brain tumor and vertigo, I was struggling to keep my real estate business while looking to make a career change. A friend and I decided to go into business as partners. I did not do any homework, because *I assumed she knew more about running a business than I did.* My new partner panicked when we did not see an immediate return; she pulled her funding and the business folded. *I had agreed to provide a personal guarantee to secure the lease and equipment, since I thought I was the high-risk partner.*

I lost my home, my vehicle, and my bank account. I was surprised that my business partner, whom I had relied on for direction, did not know that most new businesses take six months or more to net a return. I learned not to assume that a person with upper management experience knows how to start a business.

I thought that my partner was taking a big risk on me, since I knew nothing about building, running, and sustaining a business. I did not challenge her ideas or spending habits. I took her direction without question, thinking that I needed to learn about developing a business and she was my teacher. I had no confidence in myself. I felt that I had no right to question her and that all I had to contribute was the personal guarantee. She was putting up the capital to open the business, and all I had was the idea and the plan.

When this company folded, I began looking for work to supplement my real estate business, which was still struggling. I applied for work at every opportunity—restaurants, retailers, property management—but was consistently told I was overqualified.

I was accumulating debt as the desk fees at my real estate office grew and my income decreased. I was meditating every day, praying for something to work out, and feared that I would end up homeless and living on the streets, just as I had as a kid. When an opportunity presented itself, I was overjoyed, convinced this was an answer to my prayers. The offer included an apartment and came with an income. I quickly accepted with much gratitude. I thought this was a reward for continuing to show faith in my source. It was now late October 1993, if my memory is correct.

As I packed up my belongings and made arrangements to go, using money I had borrowed to hire movers, I was feeling on top of the world, *confident that my luck had finally changed and that the craziness of the past few years was now behind me.*

The movers were booked to pick up my belongings in the late morning. I was living in a rented home, so I could no longer stay. The movers called to say they would be delayed an hour, then another hour, and another hour. They finally arrived at 11:00 p.m. I suggested they unload the next day, since it was late and they were tired. I had warned them that I was moving to the top floor of a walk-up building with no elevator. They said they had pickups the next morning and needed to deliver my belongings that night. We arrived at the new apartment around 1:00 a.m. The movers brought the first few loads up the four flights of stairs. I was sorting and helping keep the path clear for them as they arrived. When a period of time passed and they brought nothing more up, I looked from the balcony to see if they were taking a break. To my shock, there was no truck in sight and my belongings were strewn all over the road in front of the property. Thankfully, friends answered my call at 2:00 a.m. and came to help me haul my belongings into the apartment. *My furniture and other belongings did not want to move into this apartment.* We laughed in sheer exhaustion at the thought that anyone would leave a single woman in such a predicament. I was appreciative of such great friends.

I settled into my new home, but after a few short months, I realized that I had been set up to take the fall in a shell game-style scam. *I was left devastated and feeling like a fool.*

I could now see that I was a great target. Nearly bankrupt, advertising to everyone that I was looking for work, I was the perfect candidate for a con man.

Whenever I felt stuck or confused, I would meditate. I searched for answers, trying to figure out what to do. *My fear was that if I exposed these swindlers and walked away, I would experience my greatest failure, being homeless, and if I stayed, I would lose my* integrity. *Since I could not live with myself if I were being dishonest and knowingly remained a part of this scam,* I was left with no other choice than to be homeless. My greatest fear was now a reality and *it was confirmed that I had failed. A great way to celebrate my fortieth birthday!* My friends helped me move my belongings into a friend's garage; one friend offered me a foam mat on the floor of a bedroom, shared with her niece. I had no choice but to give up my real estate license, since I could not afford the dues required each spring and I was creating a sizable amount of debt.

I was amazed at how my friends pulled together to help. I was feeling cared for and loved, and I was very grateful. As you will see, this gratitude became a sense of obligation and ended up teaching me another great lesson.

This strange event taught me much about who I believed myself to be. At the time, I thought that because I was committed to meditating every day, opportunities that presented themselves would automatically be good ones. Looking back, I seemed to have thought the universe, God, my higher power, was screening my career possibilities and restricting the negative ones. I blindly trusted this new partnership, even after closing a business a short time earlier because I did not do my homework when selecting a partner. This is why I spent so much time in the school of hard knocks. I did not even entertain the idea that I could know more than anyone else, so I automatically defaulted to trusting anyone and everyone. I assumed that when I meditated, I was observing and listening to my spiritual mind. It never occurred to me that the ego mind and the spiritual mind both presented thoughts and that through my free will, I could choose which thought I accepted. I did not recognize the difference between a positive, loving thought (spirit) and a negative thought (ego).

I thought I would be viewed as a fool for having bought into this con game and that if I exposed these people and walked away, I would be the tarnished one. These were negative thoughts that eroded my confidence. I thought that walking away from a home and my employment over mere ethics would confirm I was a failure, a loser, and a fool. These thoughts were my ego thoughts, and I could not see them for what they were.

The universe, our source, is amazing. My furniture and belongings did not want to move into this new home, and I saw that as the joke. After all, the higher power does not communicate through furniture, does it? I considered this the crazy thought, not my idea that I was jinxed and undeserving of anything more! If I was braver, I would have trusted the message of the furniture and been prepared when I discovered I was dealing with criminals. I learned from this that when we believe ourselves to be worthless, we will attract people who will not value or respect us. We will become targets of those who are not honest, accountable, or ethical. Too often we look to these people for leadership, thinking they have the answers and the opportunities. I never considered that my ego was holding me back, once again setting me up for a loss. My ego thoughts were again validated, since my greatest fear, being homeless, was now a reality.

In the spring of 1994, I was homeless and unemployed, applying for work with no success. Finally, I had an opportunity to take over a route for someone who was delivering the *Globe and Mail* newspaper from midnight to 4:00 a.m. To do this, I needed a car, and a kind friend allowed me to buy a vehicle on monthly payments. This work was six days a week and paid roughly three hundred dollars a month after expenses. *I was grateful for this job and gave it my best.* The managers were disappointed when I gave notice and quit. *To this day, I refer to people we call homeless as people in transition, since this can happen to any of us at any time and it is a temporary place in our lives.*

Delivering papers every night and continuing to apply for new work, I was wiser about checking things out before jumping in, since I had learned *that people who appear needy are often targeted by those looking for patsies. I was content, pleased with myself for choosing my integrity, and convinced this was why my friends had pitched in to help.*

One morning I received a call from a gentleman wanting to change the use of a property. He acknowledged that I had a lot of experience in this area and he wanted to hire me to assist him in this process. I was stunned! I said yes and gave him my price, saying I needed 50 percent in advance. He asked me the name of my company so he could write a check. Although I had many years of experience in this profession, I had never considered creating a company that provided consulting in this capacity. Realizing this man's genuine desire to hire me, on the spur of the moment and off the top of my head, I came up with a company name. He wrote the check, I opened a bank account, and my company was born. That was in July 1994. In August 1998, I incorporated this company and we are still going strong.

I knew that this company was a thank-you gift for choosing to maintain my integrity that night when I was faced with homelessness, my greatest fear. I was grateful beyond words. The sense of obligation that came from gratitude taught me some tough lessons.

Note how my thoughts were now focused on the positive. I was grateful for the paper route and aware that those who are homeless are simply in transition and not defective. I understood that feeling needy made me a target, and I felt empowered and respected for having chosen my integrity over my fear of homelessness. I felt rewarded with the creation of this company, as if it were a thank-you gift for my willingness to do what was right, even in the face of my greatest fear. Becoming grateful beyond words led me to more lessons that showed me I was not valuing myself enough. I did not realize that even with this new awareness, my ego thoughts were dominant, keeping me off balance and confused.

The business was growing by leaps and bounds. Yearly increases in volume, often 150 percent, were sending us off the charts. I was honored as a Woman of Vision by the Global TV Network and the local YMCA in the category of entrepreneurship. I felt like royalty for a day. There was great fanfare—the red carpet, the green room, interviews by graduating students. *I felt on top of the world.* In 2002, I was traveling frequently and saving a good amount of money each month. Having staff now, I enjoyed the freedom of focusing on the development of my seminar company, where my heart wanted to be. I was regularly invited to speak to women's groups and at business luncheons. I developed a series of programs that supported people searching to find themselves. Just as I was beginning to market these programs, after having invested a substantial amount of money and time, I discovered that a longtime employee, whom I took a chance on after she had been fired from her last job, was sabotaging my company.

I was distracted and not giving attention to my consulting company. *My heart was with my new seminar business.* Consulting in this capacity was something I knew well, because I had been involved in the business since I was twenty-two. It was easy to fall back on this work when I needed to regroup. My company lawyer informed me that this employee in all likelihood had counsel on how to sabotage the company and had slipped through every legal loophole. I came close to losing the business that year. This employee worked very hard to discredit me and my company, but despite this, the business became stronger. In the spring of 2003, however, my accountant passed away. He was an old-fashioned guy who did things manually. His partner, who did personal taxes and was not familiar with corporate taxes, made an error, and I had to pay more than $20,000 in personal taxes and another $14,000 in goods-and-services taxes that had not been calculated properly. I appealed the personal tax filing and was refunded a good portion, *but this all added up to stress and the feeling that I was being attacked by life.* It took better than five years to repay the corrected goods-and-services amount to Revenue Canada, which instead of appreciating the hard work it took for us to pay this debt, chose to fine the company another $3,000 for taking too long to clear up what was owed.

With all this, it did not take long for me to use up my savings, since I had only a few great years after starting the company before I faced a drop in revenue due to this sabotage. By the end of 2003, the company was more than $80,000 in debt. *I felt the gift of this company had become an albatross. It was draining me emotionally and financially. My confidence was eroding with each event. My time meditating decreased and became almost nonexistent. I felt beaten, confused, and exhausted.*

I spent December of that year in Mexico, trying to sort out what had happened *and why the rug seemed to have been pulled out from under me. I lost all confidence in my ability to judge people and make decisions. I was hurt, feeling betrayed and was unsure what to do next. I thought I was on the road to putting past nightmares behind me, so why had I failed?* My conclusion after thirty-two days in Mexico, thinking, meditating, and journaling, was that *I was not capable of being a competent business owner and that I could not be successful if I continued to do this alone.*

After my return to Canada, lacking the confidence that I was competent enough to run the company on my own, I offered the office manager the option of becoming my business partner, expecting that she would purchase shares in the company. A year later, before executing this option, I learned that she was telling my clients and staff that I was no longer the owner and that they needed to do business with her. She left shortly after I terminated several of the staff against her wishes. *I was once again faced with a mess and needed to get control of my company and my reputation.* This time I decided to choose a male business partner. This arrangement turned out to be even worse and did not last long. *I was now convinced beyond a doubt that I was the worst judge of character ever born! I understood that what we manifest is what is true for us, and since I consistently manifested betrayal and relationships in which I was not respected or valued, I took this to mean that this was true for me.*

This being my reality, I held on more tightly to my consulting business and gave up on my dream of doing seminars. *Who was I to help anyone else when I couldn't even get my own life in order? I was in debt, living on credit, pretending I was happy and successful, but filled with fear that people would find out I was stupid when it came to business.* I knew the consulting business, but it seemed no one valued what I had to say enough to want to pay for my help. I was invited to speak to industry professionals and at numerous conferences. I wrote a book and a column in the local newspaper for several years, and everyone wanted to pick my brain and get my opinion, but when I wanted to charge a fee, people said they could not afford to pay for advice. I soldiered on but was rarely able to draw a salary. When I did, it was a minimal amount, since the company and the staff came first. For eight years, I lived off the little I had left in my savings and on my credit cards. I sold my real estate holdings and scaled back my expenses so I could manage. That was a grand total of eight years working day and night, giving all I had and not being paid. *I felt I had no choice but to rescue the company, since if I closed the company I had nothing of value to offer. My identity and personal value were found in my company. I did not exist as a person. I had no awareness that this was how I viewed myself.*

In 2007, the company had finally recovered from the $80,000 debt, but late that year and through 2009, as the economy crashed and sales tanked, we once again struggled to keep the doors open. I have the most dedicated and amazing staff in the world, and these employees agreed to cut their wages to help the business survive. There was no way I could let them down and close the doors, so *they got paid and I lived off the sale of my final investment property.* I then spent thousands of dollars from my savings to launch a new service, and *I lost more money, more time, and more self-confidence. I concluded that the majority of people will not pay to solve their problems. People believe that they are entitled to be saved by someone else, and this belief is stronger than their desire to take action.* Faced with this reality while trying to develop the new service, I learned a few more big lessons. An old friend reappeared, the woman who took me in and found space for me on her bedroom floor when I was homeless so many years earlier. She said that she was finding her job difficult because the physical demands were affecting her health and that she was looking for a change. I said that I was looking to assemble a team to introduce this new concept, and she was excited. Knowing she had no experience in this field but *feeling I owed her for having taken me in,* I agreed to pay her the salary she needed to leave her job and join my team as a trainee. I was thrilled that I was able to repay her and believed she deserved this break, since she was such a kind woman and good friend. She was aware that I was funding this project completely from my limited savings and that the project would never come to fruition without outside investors coming on board. For more than a year, I paid her a full salary (not a trainee's pay) from my savings.

The two gentlemen brought in to develop the investment offering for the project turned out to be incompetent even though I had done my homework and checked them out. I had no option but to let them go, and with this, there was no more time or money to continue with the plan. I shared these facts with my friend, and she agreed to stay on, making arrangements to cover her expenses until we could launch the service. We had scaled down the project, and with close to two years of testing the program and with twelve pilot clients, who were providing favorable feedback, we felt it was now a matter of marketing on a smaller scale and building as we went.

A few months later, after a disagreement, the woman quit. She then hired lawyers, filed a grievance with the labor bureau, encouraged people to stop working with me, and cautioned clients that I was not to be trusted, telling them I did not pay as I promised. She did everything she could to force me to pay her for the months she chose to continue to work on this project after she knew the money had run out. She was cruel and ungrateful and I *felt betrayed*. I was shocked, since it was her decision to stay on and her decision to quit. I paid her a wage that she told me was what it would take to cover her living expenses while learning the business. She was not paid as an employee in training. In fact, she was paid more than I was, and *I did not mind, since I felt I owed her for helping me when I was homeless*.

In my fear-based thinking, I concluded that her act of kindness toward me back in 1993–94 was so valuable that I owed her everything I could possibly give her. *I gave her everything and I learned that it was not enough and that as soon as I had no more to give, I was cast away like old news*. Using exercise six and sifting through the negative thoughts surrounding this loss, *I discovered that I was so out of balance that I was willing not only to bankrupt myself, but to bankrupt my company in the name of saying thanks to someone I felt I owed*. Applying the process in exercise six to this situation, I discovered that my problem was rooted in *being overly grateful to anyone who helped me. I desperately needed someone to care about me. I was trying to buy friendships and relationships out of fear that if I did not have something big to offer, no one would want me.* This revelation was valuable information, and I vowed never to do this again. I am still a generous person. The difference is that the expectation and the exchange must be appropriate.

How many of these thoughts were negative, ego-based thoughts? I was shocked when I realized just how often I was listening to negative ego thoughts. I was horrified that this was how my own ego viewed me! Once we know better, we do better, so onward I went, determined to reprogram my ego data. Applying the exercises I have shared, I got serious about reprogramming my ego data, and the results did not take long to appear in my life.

Shortly thereafter, my consulting company gained strength as business picked up. After many years of being unable to draw a salary and of carrying debt, I am now being paid regularly and the company is again operating with a profit.

During all the drama and confusion, I was faithfully meditating and applying the process in exercise six that I shared in chapter 9. I would search for negative thoughts in all the events and experiences that I had, and as you can see, there were many. Several others are recorded in my journal, forever reminding me of how easy it is to be consumed by these negative thoughts. I applied this process to any hint of a negative thought, and to my surprise, after doing this for only a few months, the barrier broke, revealing to me the many legs that grew from each negative thought and awareness that I had accepted as true for me.

Applying this process, I discovered that my ego was feeding my mind these thoughts in response to my emotionally charged state. I woke up and emerged from the fog that I had been in since 2002 when the company was first sabotaged. I realized that my ego was presenting the awareness that I was a poor judge of character, that I made poor decisions when my money or time was running out, that I was obligated to those who showed me any kindness. I was overwhelmed when I realized that I had listened to these negative thoughts for nine years. I was shocked that I had taken the attempt by an employee to destroy my company as a personal attack. The problem, in fact, was someone else's lack of ethics. I had accepted this event as the proof I had sought to confirm that the fears of my childhood and the criticisms I heard then were true. Seeing that these words still evoked the pain they did when I as a child, I understood that this was because they were so emotionally charged at the time. To realize that they remained in my awareness of who I was made me take a hard look at the thoughts I was hearing. How could I entertain as true my ego's thoughts that I would never amount to anything, that I was stupid and a foolish dreamer?

Knowing that I think things through and that many of my dreams had become a reality broke the spell of my ego thoughts. I realized that my belief in myself as a competent and caring person was so fragile that it took only one simple event to revive the fears I thought had dispelled years ago. I also realized that it had taken almost ten years to regain my perspective, to accept that my ego was still reminding me of the pain of my childhood. This made me sit up and pay attention. I became more determined than ever to figure out what it took to permanently remove these negative thoughts from my awareness. I understood that it was important to listen to my thoughts and never to assume that they were always good for me. I had to select with care the thoughts that I accepted as being the real me, the me I can be, and the me I love to be. With this awareness, I was able to see the limiting beliefs I had inscribed on each of the bars in my personal prison, and as I removed them, I became completely free to be who I am.

Thanks to the process in exercise six, I was able to step back and observe my ego thoughts, which I captured on paper and recorded in my journals. As I did this, I sometimes found it shocking to learn how much I was surrendering myself to my ego mind without challenge or question.

Over these very few months, as I reviewed pages of notes filled with my negative thoughts, I learned that my ego would encourage me to immediately prepare for the worst the moment I made a decision. Because I was focusing my energy doing this, I would attract the worst-case scenario every time. I was able to revisit my relationships, both personal and professional, and see how being prepared for the worst resulted in many losses and disappointments. I walked away, jumped to assumptions, and was unbending, all because I was prepared for the worst to happen, which it did, time and time again. I was amazed to see how good I was at manifesting exactly what I believed or expected would happen. This gave me a new understanding of the phrase "Thoughts are things" and I felt empowered.

As I revisited many aspects of my life, I could see how I set myself up. For example, because I was expecting my funds to be limited, they were, and because I knew I was a poor judge of character, questionable people flocked to me. Because I was indebted to anyone who was kind, I became emotionally and financially bankrupt. It all made sense. The pieces fell into place, and when the fog lifted, it was clear that I was living an ego-based life. My energy and attention were being given to my ego mind. It was louder and quicker to respond than my spirit mind. Because my inner self speaks softly, gently, and kindly and my ego mind had me convinced that I did not deserve such treatment, I did not respond to my genuine self with the same energy and emotion that I gave my ego thoughts.

When I understood that these were negative thoughts automatically brought to my attention by my ego, I was shocked and appalled that my own ego was sabotaging me. The problem wasn't my friends or the world out there, but me and only me. Instantly I could see how these negative thoughts and external influences, collected to define who I was, had infiltrated every aspect of my life—friends, family, career, relationships, money, and love. I was never unwanted or unworthy; it was my ego that would not let me see past the pain and fear that accumulated as a child. This child compared herself to the rest of the world, with her child's mind, and concluded that there was something wrong with her. Still, I was not angry at my ego or myself for allowing this to go on for more than fifty years. I was too excited about finally seeing the truth. I understood at last that these negative, limiting things that I believed about myself were only the thoughts my ego was programmed to show me when I questioned myself and that none of these things I believed for so long was true.

I am courageous, kind, gentle, and compassionate. It matters to me that people are respected, and I want to help where I can without giving myself away or compromising who I am. I no longer set myself up to be harmed or to feel that I need to apologize to those who consider my ideas foolish just because no one else agrees with them. I could not be angry at my ego, since it is a part of who I am. I was the one who lost perspective and allowed myself to live in the shadows, hiding from my pain and pretending my fears were not real.

I now know that real balance in life comes from dancing in harmony with your ego. We are out of balance when we are out of step with who we are or when we deny that we are valuable. The dance keeps us alive and creates our experiences. It is who we are as an individual "I am" that makes each of us unique.

It is important to remember that our ego is not a friend or an enemy; it is simply the storage hub that we draw from as we define our awareness, our individualized self.

I understand that the external influences of a world filled with fear, doubt, and judgment can make us feel powerless and that this can be intimidating. I understand that our internal influences are affected by these external influences more than we know. I also understand that once we open our minds and our hearts to the possibility that we are valued, that we are enough, and that we are worth knowing and loving, we gain the appropriate perspective on these influences and manifest our authentic lives. We then live freely as who we are. Our dreams become a reality. The only thing any of us needs to do to find ourselves is to answer the question, "Who am I?" We must do this with trust and faith and let go of the fear blocking what we might discover as we complete the search and escape from the cocoon.

Opening your mind to the possibility that there is more to you than you think is a great place to start the process of knowing who you are. When you connect with who you are, that void, that longing to search for more, will disappear. The pieces will fall into place and you will know yourself and confidently move in the direction of your dreams, feeling happy, humble, and content.

Chapter 12

To Be or Not to Be?

A lesson that Bernice has learned along the way:
If you're lying in a hospital bed looking at the monitor
that is recording your vital signs, you want to see peaks
and valleys, not a flat line. Get excited about those
curves that life throws you—those peaks and valleys.
It means you're alive and still in the game!

—Robert Allen and Mark Victor Hansen,
Cash in Flash

"To be or not to be: that is the question." Why has this question touched so many at the core? Shakespeare's line speaks to the choice to live or to die, but until recently, I did not realize that it is not simply about being alive or dead, but about choosing to be a participant in your life. I did not understand the wisdom in this question and ask myself if I would be who I was meant to be.

This is the ultimate choice we must make, whether to be defined by our ego mind or by the wisdom of our genuine self. That is the question! This famous line in Shakespeare's *Hamlet* makes complete sense to me for the first time.

Which part of you shows up in your awareness when you are asked who you are—the self you know to be genuine or the self that your ego thinks you are?

In the last two chapters we explored external and internal influences to learn how these affect our personal awareness. We can see that outside influences, supporting our negative thoughts, become internal influences once we accept them as true. Once they are programmed into our ego, we act on these beliefs each time a situation calling for that data occurs.

It is important to understand that not all propaganda is negative. When your ego is programmed with information in line with your internal knowing, your genuine self, you will discover that this information enhances who you know yourself to be. Your ego will become less susceptible to replacing the new data with negative data as long as you are willing to take charge of what you accept as true for you and no longer allow old, negative information time in your mind. This is not a difficult task once you become confident in being and expressing who you genuinely are. It is quite a lot of fun to see both perspectives and choose which you want to experience.

The process is not about being perfect, winning a prize, being right all the time, or being better than everyone else. This is about getting up each day happy to be you, enjoying the life you have and looking forward to whatever is around the corner. Being aware of the things that can influence you from the external world and from within yourself gives you the choice of seeing the bigger picture or remaining limited by the awareness that you have available in your ego. If you are looking for a missing piece or to fill a void, then the search is an internal one. The solutions to these deeply personal needs and wants are not found outside of yourself.

When I reflect on my life, I can see that I lost time with my mother and gave up on relationships that had great potential. I overlooked opportunities for careers and said no to experiences I would have loved to try, all because my ego thoughts were so much louder than my genuine-self thoughts. Because I so often doubted myself, my ego data affirmed that I was justified in having these doubts, which strengthened them, increased my lack of confidence, intensified my fear, and gave me permission to feel confused.

I blamed my parents, teachers, the government, the police, and child welfare agencies. I blamed the economy, doctors, lawyers, and society for not caring enough to help, for not taking care of me, feeling no one valued or wanted me enough to do something to let me know that I mattered. I searched every corner of the outer world, convinced that the lack of response that I expected was the evidence I needed that I did not matter, that I would never be enough, that I was of no real value, that I was unwanted and quite foolish to think this could change.

For most of my life, this is what my ego held in its awareness as the definition of who I was. This programming began with a few words spoken by my mother, a woman under more stress than we would care to imagine. Being a typical child, I internalized these words and interpreted them from my child's point of view. Because these words were charged with a child's emotion, they were imbedded in my ego database. A child's ego does not rationalize any more than an adult's ego does, so mine simply held on to the facts that I accepted as truths and they became my beliefs about who I was.

My mother began telling me that I was useless when I was as young as three. When I was a small child, she expected me to do tasks appropriate for girls in their teens, such as ironing, cooking, cleaning, and night feedings of siblings. I accepted her statement as a truth about me, since I had no awareness that these were not reasonable tasks for me at that age. As she apologized to strangers for my skinny body and for teeth too big for my mouth and said, "We don't know what happened to Bernice," I concluded I was the ugly duck of the family. When she told me that no man would ever want me because I cried and scared easily, I assumed she was correct. She told me it was my fault she married my dad, and though I did not understand what this meant, I knew that I owed her because I was the cause of her pain and unhappiness. I internalized these hurtful and confusing statements. These became the foundation for defining who I was. When I began questioning them as an adult, I would be reminded of the pain and fear of past experiences, and I then attracted new experiences that would support the foundation present in my ego mind.

My mother has called me her heartless daughter for as long as I can remember. About two years ago, she sent me a lovely card with beautiful flowers on the front, and as I read the words she wrote inside I cried so hard I could not drive for about twenty minutes. She said, "My only regret in life is that I did not put you up for adoption. Maybe if I had, you would have not grown up to be so heartless." Do you have any idea how much my ego loved that one? I had evidence that she was cruel and relentlessly so. At that moment, I vowed never speak to her again and never to accept mail from her. To me, she was dead. I had no mother.

This one card gave my ego so much data to support the idea that my mother did not want me that I could not see beyond the pain. This card said that I was right; I had been shortchanged.

Who was I to think I could beat all this and be healthy and happy, expecting to feel wanted and loved? Such thinking was one of those fantasies that my mother always said would cause me nothing but disappointment. She often told me that one of my problems was that I set my standards too high and that I was not realistic in my expectations. I recall asking her just how low I should set my standards. Until I learned to apply the process I shared in exercise six, I had no idea that my life was lived based on beliefs that were outrageously false.

If you want to test this process, take any of the negative statements that my mother made and apply them to the eight steps. You will discover as I did that not one is absolutely true for any human being. By rejecting thoughts that supported my mother's statements so many years before and becoming aware of each negative root in my belief system, I soon began feeling the changes in my body, mind, and spirit. I was coming to life as if I had been in a fog or frozen state for a decade or more. With these changes bringing a new clarity and a new perspective on who I was and the journey I had taken, I soon realized that my mother's message was that she felt she had failed me and regretted not letting me go to another family that may have done better than she could and made me happy. The truth was that this card was an expression of her love for me, not her hate. I could not see this until I pulled back the black veil of negative thoughts that my ego had placed around me, supported with years of data. This data included numerous people who felt my mother was a monster who should never have had kids. I can always find people who agree that with my history, I should have these challenges. Many people are willing to commiserate with me when I feel shortchanged. Only a very few friends have pointed out that my mother was trying to apologize and say she loved me with the card.

I do not approve of or endorse child abuse of any kind, mental, physical, spiritual, or sexual. I oppose any act that diminishes a child's right to express himself age appropriately. Children are resilient and so are adults, but that does not mean we need to push them to the max to see what they are made of. Remember that the cages limiting us are etched with beliefs rooted in the information received as children. Every word spoken in anger or without thought can scar a child for many years, so I challenge all parents, grandparents, and caregivers to be thoughtful in choosing their words around children.

I hold no ill feeling toward anyone in my past, including my mother. It is sad that she feels such guilt at this stage of her life, since her guilt is unwarranted. I see now how it took courage for her not to run away, to stay in an environment where she was neglected and regularly beaten by a drunken man; she was hungry, frightened, with limited funds and no support. She worked hard-labor jobs for minimum wages and often would find the bank accounts cleaned out when her husband, my father, needed a drink or wanted to party and impress his friends. I remember coming home from school and finding all the furnishings had been gambled away. I recall being woken up in the middle of the night as the police hauled dad to jail, mom to the hospital after he had beaten her, and us kids to a shelter. These events were her life, but she did not give up. Just like any mother, she wanted her kids to have the best. She was tormented when she could not provide Christmas gifts and new school clothes, and her angry words, especially about men being unreliable and useless, were true in her experience. I think that in her own way she wanted us to be prepared so we would not be abused as she was. In any case, I do not feel she has been judged fairly by society, by her children, or by her own definition of herself. She is in her late eighties and lives in a world filled with guilt and concern over having lost so much of her memory. This is a sad thing, since she did the best she could with what she knew and with the resources available.

Why we as adults choose to hold any parent responsible for choices we have made since leaving their care is beyond comprehension; yet this is what the negative propaganda supports as the norm. The sad part is that by accepting this propaganda, we are depriving ourselves of feeling the love of our parents—in my case, my mother. No, she is not and never has been a storybook mother, but I am grateful that I figured out the truth while she is still alive and I look forward to getting to know her. She cried when I told her that I thought she was courageous for having stuck it out and that I knew she loved my dad and held on to the hope he would change. She is forever apologizing, wishing she could have done things differently, and I hope she hears me say that all she needs to do is enjoy being alive. I told her that since her youngest child is over forty, she is no longer responsible for the choices her children make as adults. Her response was that she looked forward to her death, since life had been really hard and that she regretted not remembering much anymore. That breaks my heart, especially knowing that her life has been one of enduring pain and fear.

I am grateful that she was who she was, since this led me to figure out who I am. One of those negative propaganda claims is that people need to hit bottom before they look to change. In keeping with that thought, I was born at rock bottom; therefore, I had only one direction in which to go. I fell, skinned my knees, and picked myself up because there was no one there to protect me. I learned early that if it was to be, it was up to me. It me took a lifetime to understand that who I am is inside myself, not encased outside in some defined persona that does not exist. I listened, learned, explored, and questioned, and I find it almost comical that I spent all that time searching outside of myself, when all along I was right there, standing in my shoes. I never looked beyond the wall of fear where I hid myself, because I was afraid that I would not like who I found on the other side.

I peeked beyond that black wall, and to my surprise, the fear disappeared and the view on the other side is everything and more than what I had dreamed it would be.

To be or not to be? For me, the answer is nothing less than to be! To be me, confidently, proudly, and wholly—in step with my desires, in the flow of my life, and in harmony with my genuine self as I dance through each day with my ego.

Chapter 13

DARE TO BELIEVE

*Don't live down to expectations. Go out
there and do something remarkable.*

—Wendy Wasserstein

In January 2012, I took an eighteen-day cruise from Los Angeles to Hawaii. I needed to be with myself, my newly found self, the me I had ignored and repressed for fifty-seven years. I had no idea that I would make so many changes to my life when I returned. I have gotten past the anger of being betrayed and taken advantage of by so many people whom I had wanted to help. I am no longer embarrassed or ashamed that it took me fifty-seven years to get over my childhood and to fall in love not only with myself, but with my mother. If I ever run into the gal who sabotaged my company, I will thank her for giving me the opportunity to find out how to protect a business and for the lessons I learned about the personal cost of being a rescuer. She has been a great teacher in my life, and although I do not respect her ethics, I thank her for the lessons she taught me.

My company is stronger than it has been in years. My staff, friends, and family are amazing. I finally found the words that allowed me to put this experience on paper. I am looking forward to helping whomever I can, however I can. My only mission is to help people looking for more to find it by being who I am when I'm in their company.

I can't help but reflect on the wonder of it all as I recall how a little girl who stuttered and was so shy she was afraid of her own shadow grew into a woman who one day stumbled onto an opportunity not only to develop a company, but to pioneer and create an entire new service. The company, which evolved out of a simple phone call from a man needing help with a project, is thriving almost twenty years later.

I have always believed this company came to me as a thank-you gift for having the integrity not to take advantage of people who weren't interested in the details of their investments. The company has weathered more stormy days than most people could imagine and has grown stronger despite the challenges. As the sole founder and owner, I have been blessed for these past eighteen years with the gifts of learning what it takes to earn respect, to roll with the punches, to turn the other cheek, and most of all, to look beyond what appears to be real. I recall many times feeling the frustration of knowing the consulting business is not what excites me, that my passion is to see others blossom into who they are. If I can help people achieve this even in a small way, I am happy, satisfied, and beyond pleased with who I am.

The big message of this grand experience is never to let go of that dream. Don't just dare to dream; dare to dream big. Go for the star, the big prize. For me, that meant never letting go of the conviction that one day I would know what it was like to be wanted, to be enough, to be valued, and to be loved. Although the journey that got me here appears to have been a rough and frightening one, I would do it again in a minute to have these results.

Now that I have arrived and I reflect back on every tear, every doubt, and every moment of wondering if I was crazy, I can honestly say the prize of knowing who I am was worth it. I am at home in my own skin, and I enjoy being my genuine self, a person fully engaged in this world. I have no worries or fears of loss. I have no insecurities or doubts that I can achieve whatever I desire. I don't know how many more hours, days, or years I will be on this planet, but I do know I will continue to cherish each moment that I am blessed to receive. I thank you for taking this journey with me in the pages of this book, and I dare you to believe in yourself, to believe in your dreams, and to believe you can have it all.

When you dance in harmony with your ego, you are no longer limited by the ego's awareness. You are in balance with all aspects of your being, your ego, and the spirit within you.

Summary of Exercises

~~~~~~~~~~~~~~~~

I have pulled the exercises from each chapter for easy reference. I would love to hear your results. You can find me through my website, berniewinterseminars@gmail.com.

CHAPTER 6

EXERCISE ONE

Set up your private sanctuary. Create that special place where you feel surrounded by love, with scents and treasures that you have handpicked because they bring you joy.

EXERCISE TWO

Complete the statements:

I am _____. I am _____. I am

_____.

I want to be _____

_____.

Chapter 7

Exercise Three: the six steps
to finding your passion

1. Identify how much time you spend searching for your purpose and for your passion.

2. Ask yourself if you are undertaking this search to learn something you really want to know or something you feel you should know.

3. Make a list of at least ten things that you love to do.

4. Do one of these things at least three times each week, and give these activities your full attention while doing them.

5. Track an activity for a minimum of three months and record what you did and how you felt during and after. If you felt great, continue doing it. If an activity brought you stress, anxiety, or frustration, do something else for three months, again tracking your feelings. Continue this process for all items on your list.

6. Incorporate into your life on a consistent basis those activities that brought you joy or a sense of wellness.

This exercise will help you identify the things you are passionate about and connect you to them. When an activity makes you feel excited, calm, peaceful, proud, loving, big-hearted, thrilled, happy, strong, light, invincible, courageous, or so pleased you want to shout from a rooftop, you have found your passion. Watch for things that you do in everyday life that produce any of these feelings. It could be walking the dog, admiring a room you just cleaned, jogging on a beach, or fixing a fence. It could be completing a project or achieving a major goal. Whatever it is, make note and strive to incorporate activities that make you feel good into each day. Start with three times each week for ninety days and then increase the frequency to four days a week, five, six, and seven. You will agree that life is pretty grand when your week is filled with things you love to do. When you have one of those days that I call "sideways days," when things don't go as you would like, return to your list and remember that tomorrow is another day. (I use the term *sideways days* because I believe there are no bad days. Each day's experience brings more information about who I am and how I am doing, so every day is a blessing. Sideways days are those unexpected days when the best-made plans come to nothing.)

CHAPTER 8

EXERCISE FOUR: JUDGMENTS

1. List the judgments you have for others in the areas of career, relationships, health, mind (attitude), and body.

2. List the expectations you have for yourself in these areas.

3. Compare this list with the list of your characteristics and goals for who you want to be. Identify those that are not congruent with your genuine-self desires.

4. For the next twenty-one days, do one of the things on your genuine-self list of desires each day as often as you can. For example. if one of your desired characteristics

is to be kind, for the next twenty-one days, do at least one new kind thing each day. Do this for all the action items on the list and watch how quickly the programming of your ego changes and the actions become automatic. Your new actions are what your ego will bring to your awareness in response.

For any judgment that you have discovered, take the same approach, with one difference. Instead of taking an action step for twenty-one days, find twenty-one reasons your judgment is not accurate. For example, you may judge that you don't need a man, since they are all self-centered and egotistical, with no respect for women. List twenty-one examples of the opposite. You may start by acknowledging that you need a man to open a pickle jar or to help change a tire. It is important to list only the items that you believe to be true. Listing what you think are politically correct reasons will only feed your ego incorrect data. You may find this to be one of the most difficult assignments, because when we have faith that our beliefs are true, it is not easy to accept alternate possibilities. In any case, it is more than worth the time to do this exercise.

5. Repeat this process with all the items on your judgments list. It will get easier as you complete the lists.

Chapter 9

Exercise Five: storyboard visualization

Visualize yourself as vital, the perfect size for your body type, glowing, strong, and doing the things that you love to do. Visualize this ideal self every day. Create a storyboard with all the fashions, colors, activities, foods, and other things that you love. Build this storyboard around your vision of your healthy self. Put the storyboard in a place where you can see it, possibly in your sanctuary or private space, and study it. Feel the pleasure it brings, then close your eyes, and see it come to life in your mind. Invite your imagination to taste the foods, touch your favorite outfit, and feel how well it fits your body. Do the activities as you are in this space, and wrap your arms around yourself as you feel the joy and wonder of being there. Make the commitment to do this exercise as often as you can in a week. The more often you do this, the sooner you will feel the changes happening deep within as your old ego programming is replaced with the new data about who you are.

EXERCISE SIX

The following questions will assist you in determining whether your desires and beliefs are coming from the data bank of your ego or from your genuine-self desire. These questions will bring clarity to issues you face and help you discover whether you are listening to your ego or your authentic self. You will no longer be affected by hypnotic factors and will make the choices that best serve you. Follow this eight-step process.

Step 1. Statement: I _____

2. Is this statement true? Spiritually, mentally, physically, and emotionally the absolute truth with no exceptions or other possibilities? Yes or no?

3. If the answer is yes, that your statement is the absolute truth and you respond or act accepting that it is the truth, then you feel …

4. If the answer is no, that your statement is not the absolute truth and you respond or act accepting that it is not the truth, then you feel ...

5. Which of these two choices made you feel empowered and pleased with having respected yourself? (Observe how great it feels to accept the truth about this situation. You chose which option to accept, the absolute truth or the excuses disguised as truths, and benefited by being empowered when honoring what is true.)

6. I accept that my statement blocked me from seeing the truth by ...

7. What action(s) will I take when a thought blocks me from hearing my genuine self?

8. My genuine self and my ego self now know that the reality of this issue is that ...

CHAPTER 10

EXERCISE SEVEN: NOTE THOUGHTS
THAT RESONATE WITH YOU

Review the ten external influences covered in chapter 9 and take note of any thoughts that resonate with you. Take note, too, of your emotions and any physical reactions such as chills or warm feelings. Determine whether this information makes you feel stronger, happier, positive, excited, sad, weak, or some other way.

If you feel more energized, alert, and alive, keep those moments of joy and peace coming. Add the actions that produce these great new feelings to your daily to-do list and increase the frequency whenever possible.

Exercise Eight

Take a twenty-dollar bill and place it on a plate in the middle of your dining room table when you go to bed tonight. In the morning, when you wake up, make a list of all the things that twenty dollars did for you while you were sleeping.

Chapter 11

Exercise Nine: notations of negative thinking, my internal influences

1. I did not do any homework, because I assumed she knew more about running a business than I did.

2. I agreed to the personal guarantee, because I thought I was the high-risk party in the partnership.

3. My furniture and my belongings did not want to move into this apartment.

4. If I exposed them and walked away, I would experience my greatest failure, being homeless, and if I stayed, I would lose my integrity.

5. I was left with no other choice but to be homeless. My greatest fear was now a reality, and it was confirmed that I had failed.

6. As I realized this, I was devastated and felt like a fool.

7. I was now convinced beyond a doubt that I was the worst judge of character ever born! I understood that what we manifest is what is true for us, and since I consistently

manifested betrayal and relationships in which I was not respected or valued, I took this to mean that this was true for me.

8. Who was I to help anyone else when I couldn't even get my own life in order?

9. I felt I had no choice, since if I closed the company I had nothing of value to offer.

10. She was not paid as a person in training; she was paid more than I drew for myself, and I did not mind, since I felt I owed her for helping me back in the days when I was homeless. In my fear-based thinking, I concluded that her act of kindness toward me in 1993–94 was so valuable that I owed her everything. I gave her everything and I learned that it was not enough, and as soon as I had no more to give I was cast away like old news. Applying the process in exercise six to this situation, I discovered that my problem was rooted in being overly grateful to anyone who helped me. I desperately needed someone to care about me and want me and felt that this was the most I could get. I was trying to buy friendships and relationships out of fear that if I did not have something big to offer no one would want me. Again, this sense of obligation that came from feeling grateful taught me some tough lessons.

11. I lost all confidence in my ability to judge people and make decisions. I was hurt, feeling betrayed and unsure what to do next. I thought I was on the road to putting my past nightmares behind me, so why had I failed?

12. My conclusion after thirty-two days in Mexico, thinking, meditating, and journaling, was that I was not capable of being a competent business owner and that I could not be trusted to go it alone.

13. I was now convinced beyond a doubt that I was the worst judge of character ever born!

14. I felt I had no choice, because if I closed the company I had nothing of value to offer.

15. Why did I feel so betrayed, attacked, and disrespected when I knew I had done all I could?

16. Again, because I trusted and did not do enough homework, I attracted two female and two male business partners who turned out to be faking their credentials. I felt like a target for con artists.

Dare to dream big! Enjoy the journey. Celebrate the changes at every step along the way as you get to know your authentic self.

Cheers!
Bernice
berniewinterseminars@gmail.com

CPSIA information can be obtained at www.ICGtesting.com
Printed in the USA
LVOW11s1252040314

375882LV00001B/7/P